HOW TO INSPECT A
HOUSE
EXPANDED EDITION

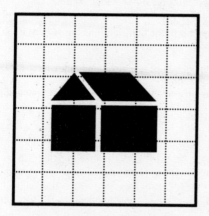

George Hoffman

with Mark C. Friedman

Addison-Wesley Publishing Company

Reading, Massachusetts Menlo Park, California New York
Don Mills, Ontario Wokingham, England Amsterdam
Bonn Sydney Singapore Tokyo Madrid San Juan
Paris Seoul Milan Mexico City Taipei

Many of the designations used by manufacturers and sellers to distinguish their products are claimed as trademarks. Where those designations appear in this book and Addison-Wesley was aware of a trademark claim, the designations have been printed in initial capital letters (i.e., Drylok).

A Note to Readers: The authors and publishers have made every effort to make sure that the information in this book ensures safety. Because the specifics of each house, environment, and materials vary greatly, neither the authors nor the publishers shall be liable for any damage that may result from the use of this book.

Library of Congress Cataloging-in-Publication Data

Hoffman, George Cleborn
      How to inspect a house / George Hoffman with Mark C. Friedman.   Expanded ed.
          p.   cm.
      Includes bibliographical references and index.
      ISBN 0-201-57708-9
        1. Dwellings–Inspection. 2. House buying. I. Friedman, Mark C.
      II. Title.
TH4817.5.H64 1992
643'.12—dc20   92-18896
                                                              CIP

Previous text revision by Steve Horgan
Cover design by Hannus Design Associates
Text design by Janis Owens
Set in 11-point Meridien by Pagesetters, Inc., Brattleboro, VT

1 2 3 4 5 6 7 8 9-MU-95949392
First printing, November 1992

Addison-Wesley books are available at special discounts for bulk purchases. For more information, please contact:

Special Markets Department
Addison-Wesley Publishing Company
Reading, MA 01867
(617) 944–3700 × 2431

Dedicated to the people who live in slopey but stable houses and have learned to serve plates with the vegetables up, the gravy down

Acknowledgments

....

I would like to express my deep gratitude to Betsy Alberti, who offered constructive criticism and editorial guidance while I worked on this book. I am also very thankful for Robert La Rose and Jerry Minton, who helped me revise the chapter on electricity, and for Raymond H. Beale, termite consultant, and Dr. Bradford Kard of the U.S. Department of Agriculture Forestry Service, who provided helpful information and review of the termite chapter. I owe a great debt to John Bell for his insightful editing, Tiffany Cobb for handling production, and the publishing staff at Addison-Wesley. Finally, and most important, we must all thank Mary Hoffman for her support in allowing us to revise her late husband's book.

M.C.F.

Contents

Introduction
to the Expanded Edition

....

For twenty years *How to Inspect a House* has been acclaimed for how well it demystifies the house inspection process. The concerns of home buyers change with time, however, so we have once again updated the book to provide answers to questions people ask today. This edition contains a new chapter on environmental hazards—such as lead paint, formaldehyde, and radon gas—that threaten the health of a homeowner's family and/or the value of a home. The house inspection checklist has been expanded to reflect these questions. In addition, the book provides information on professional inspections and how to close a deal, as well as a regular maintenance schedule that will remain useful long after you've moved in.

Despite the title *How to Inspect a House*, it was never the intention of the late George Hoffman to do away with professional home inspectors, who play a crucial role in the purchase of a house. Not only will some banks require that your future home be inspected by an expert before they will grant you a mortgage, but you also cannot get homeowner's insurance without such an inspection. But with professional inspectors charging up to $500 per inspection, it isn't possible to have each house you are considering inspected by an expert. That brings us to the purpose of this book: to enable you to do the preliminary inspections on your own. Your ability to spot flaws and/or strengths in a house will allow you to sift through your selection of homes and save the inspector for the one house that seems most promising.

Mark C. Friedman

Preface
Think Carefully When
Shopping for a Home

———————————
·······················

This book's purpose is to make clear in layman's language what you must know in order to make a physical examination of a house. When used as a guide to diagnose the physical condition of a house, this book can save a buyer thousands of dollars if faults are found, or can give him or her peace of mind to know that the purchase is sound. Homeowners may use this book to look for faults that can be corrected before they become serious.

Although home inspectors are essential in the final purchase of a house, it is not necessary to have every house you look at inspected by a costly professional. When you do decide to hire a home inspector, there are a few things you should keep in mind. Home inspectors are supposed to work *for* the buyer. Remember, the real estate agent is not the home expert. Hire a house inspector who is totally impartial. That means someone who simply inspects the house and submits his or her findings but does nothing whatsoever to correct any fault he or she may find. In that way the inspector will not be motivated to find work. The inspector should be knowledgeable enough to give approximate costs of repairs as a guide so that the client can make a decision on the house. He or she should know, for example, the cost of different kinds of roofing materials as well as the labor costs to install them. He or she should also know what new plumbing and electric wiring costs are.

When you hire a home inspector, beware of "sweetheart"

arrangements. An agent may know a friendly contractor or someone with a little experience who will look at your house. The contractor remains friendly as long as he or she makes favorable reports. You must find an independent expert.

When you stand back and look at a house, it looks like a huge, mysterious monster with numerous complexities and hidden secrets. But if you take it apart piece by piece, you can begin to understand it. In this book you will go through a typical home inspection to learn, step by step, the physical condition of the structure: that is, drainage, foundation, construction, plumbing, sewage, wiring, heating, tile, roof, paint, as well as signs of dry rot, termites, and the like. The tools needed are a steel ball of $1/2$- to $3/4$-inch diameter, a level, a screwdriver, a flashlight, an electrical tester, a mirror, a bamboo chopstick, and a good eye (Fig. 1). With these instruments and some basic knowledge, you can inspect any house and make your own preliminary evaluation.

The knowledge you gain from this book will be even more valuable if you purchase directly from the seller, who often doesn't know of faults and would be reluctant to disclose them if he or she did. If you alert the seller to these faults, he or she may even lower the asking price of the house or repair what is wrong before you purchase it.

First, think about the house and its setting and whether you want to own it. You have investigated the neighborhood for schools, number of families, shopping, convenient commuting, sunshine, possibility of expansion, taxes, and the numerous ancillary points of personal taste. Think carefully. Is there a highway nearby? How busy is it? Will it be widened and used heavily, thus creating disturbing noise? Are you pleased with the view? Will it remain as it is? Or is there a good possibility that a development will be going in to spoil your view? For some answers, call the local agency that handles zoning and community development.

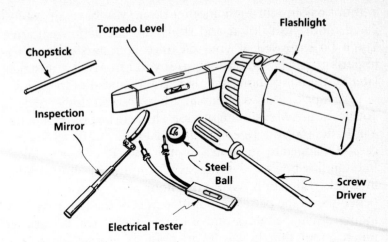

Figure 1
Inspection Tools

There are many other things to think about; their importance depends on how you think about them. You may want to know the location of the dump and the nature of the trash disposal system in the area. How about the distance to the airport or fire station and the proximity to movies, bars, or campus life? How many rental units are in the neighborhood? Is there a swimming pool on the other side of the fence next to your patio? Is your neighbor a weekend mechanic with automobiles parked all about? Are there boats and trailers cluttering the area? Chat with your future neighbors. Think now, and you might not despair later.

When you get right down to the house itself, consider some important aspects that are frequently overlooked but are as important to a house as its roof.

Take circulation, for instance. A general rule should be to keep traffic out of rooms. Corridors are for passing through to get to rooms. If there is no way to get to a certain room without passing through another room, you have an "obligated room." Sit down and study the circulation pattern. You'll be surprised at yourself once you start giving this important aspect some thought. If you can avoid a mistake later by thinking about it earlier, you're ahead of the game.

Take time to draw a floor plan; then you can study it when you get home. Measurements don't have to be precise, but do a little stepping off. Keep in mind that many traffic problems can be changed by moving a door or two. In a large room, a freestanding bookcase or massive furniture can direct traffic in another direction. With your floor plan you can trace in pencil the traffic patterns that members of the family would follow down hallways and through doors. You'll learn as much about that house in an hour as you would in six months of living in it.

Traffic problems are closely related to poor layout. Consider your family's life-style. Do you use the den for family gatherings, or does your family prefer assembling in the kitchen? If so, can dining be directly off the kitchen? Do you eat from trays while watching TV? Think about it. Would you like the bedrooms and baths to be completely private? Think about acoustic as well as visual privacy.

"Interior zoning" is a good term that describes another important aspect of layout. There are three categories of zoning: work, privacy, and shared activities. Laundering is certainly work and should have its own separate area. The kitchen is another work zone. Do you want to be alone while preparing food, or do you like to talk and visit?

Are you a reader? Can you sit and read in the living room during certain periods of the day without being interrupted by people running through? Do you have a hobby that requires privacy? Keep in mind that there are no absolute rules for the layout of a house. Every family has a different life-style. But think thrice before you buy a house that has to be completely remodeled to get a floor plan that will please you.

Think about the house's acoustics. Sit in the living room and listen. Carpeting and curtains will change how sound travels through the house, but you can still get a sense of its noise levels. Will private conversations stay private? Do footsteps on other floors bother you? Ask someone to flush a toilet or run water in the tub. Do you hear the sound of water resonating through the house, or a bang when the water is shut off? (A plumber can eliminate some of these sounds.) Sit in the bedroom and ask someone to turn on the furnace. Are these noises loud enough to disturb your sleep?

Think about safety. Check with police about neighborhood crime. Is the house isolated from the neighbors and the street? If so, thieves could break in without being seen. Make sure all doors, paths, and parking areas can be well illuminated. See that all doors and windows have good locks. Many glass sliding doors can be lifted out of their frames. If locks to prevent this are missing, you could ask that they be installed before the final purchase, or closing. Is there a burglar alarm system? Ask the owner to demonstrate it and explain how it operates. Silent alarm systems to alert police are available, but many communities don't allow direct hookups. Ask. The police urge and invite inquiries about the best kind of alarm system for the area. They are knowledgeable and eager to help.

A house must have several exterior doors strategically placed in case of fire. You should not have to run through the whole house to find an exit door. A multiple-story house must have approved fire escapes. If you are in doubt about the proper fire escapes, call the fire department. They'll check your house at no cost. Smoke detectors cannot be recommended too highly. The proper location of smoke detectors is important. A firefighter can survey a house and tell you the best kind of detector and where it should be placed. Then follow the manufacturer's installation instructions carefully.

Please give some thought to the accessibility of your home for handicapped people, taking into consideration the ease of getting about inside the house using a wheelchair or walker. We should all make our homes inviting to persons for whom mobility is a problem.

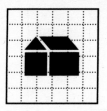

Foundation and Soil

····························

Without a good foundation, a house is not worth inspecting. We talk about foundations when we think of house support, but beneath the foundation is the footing, which is hidden (see Fig. 2). Its purpose is to distribute weight over a larger area. The footing should be deep enough to reach firm soil and have sufficient steel to give the concrete tensile strength. Cracks in foundations are frequently caused by poor footings or, in some older houses, no footing at all. Old common brick foundations had no footing as a rule, nor was there steel in them. Concrete without steel is worthless for foundations. Without steel, concrete will crack and break apart. Concrete has good compression resistance but little tensile strength. Steel wire mesh is required for concrete slabs, and in some instances steel bars must be embedded in the concrete.

On a hillside, the foundation not only should offer stability on which to build but should also act as a hill-holding barrier. This means it should extend deep enough to be below the zone of moisture change. If it doesn't and the soil is clayey, when the soil is lubricated with moisture, the foundation

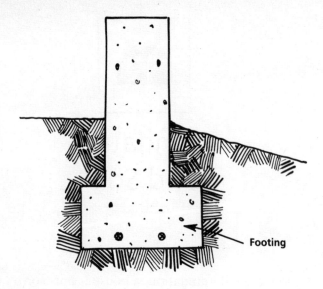

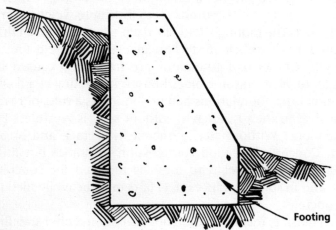

Figure 2
Footings

could slip downhill, carrying the house with it. The depth of the foundation can't be determined, so you have to look for signs that it's deep enough. Hillside houses are more and more common. And in metropolitan areas and most suburban areas, the best hillside lots have been used, so it's more risky to build on the lots that are left.

Because a foundation is only as good as the earth it's built on, a word about soil is in order. The less you modify the soil, the better your chances of preventing slides. Beware of bulldozers. Removing soil on a hillside to make a shelf is risky, for you have removed the footing of the earth above. Take a small pile of sand and remove a little at the base. What happens? You weaken the footing and the pile crumbles. No support. Geologists would say you have upset the "angle of repose." It's a good phrase, both poetic and descriptive. A hillside that has been standing for many years is at peaceful rest. Upset it and a landslide could occur as gravity works to reestablish the natural angle of repose. If you wonder whether the hillside where the house is located is a potential slide area, walk around and look for large radial cracks that run opposite to the slope. Large cracks could mean an unstable hillside. The soil may be rocky or shaley beneath the surface. It's not firm bedrock. If there's a clay layer, water could lubricate the clay and slippage could occur. Wavelike areas of earth, which show on the surface like little terraced amphitheaters, indicate minor soil slippage; how much and how deep is difficult to determine by yourself. If there are trees on the property, look them over, for if the slides were severe they will have curves in their trunks. This is because trees always strive to grow vertically. Small cracks often indicate rapid drying out of surface soil after a heavy winter rain. They'll close up come next winter. But if the soil situation is suspect, especially on a hillside, have a soil engineer check the property. The engineer should also consider what effect a new building on nearby property would have.

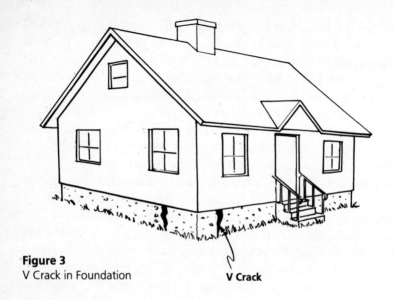

Figure 3
V Crack in Foundation   **V Crack**

V Cracks

While inspecting the foundation, check the corners, which are the weak areas. Without sufficient steel in the concrete, the corners could break. Steel helps make the foundation act as one firm unit. Figure 3 shows two cracks in a level perimeter foundation. These are **V** cracks, wider at the top than the bottom. Undoubtedly the corner of the whole structure has settled. You may find hairline cracks anywhere, but don't worry about them. It's the **V** cracks that give cause for alarm.

Figure 4 shows a crack all the way through a perimeter foundation. This is a differential settlement due to insufficient steel and/or a footing that doesn't reach solid soil.

In a hillside house with a stepped foundation (Fig. 5), A and B are the weak places, for there is less concrete and often insufficient steel. Note the large **V** cracks.

If a house is built on a hillside, chances are a shelf was cut first, earth was pushed forward, and the house was

Figure 4
Differential Settlement

anchored on the shelf but much of it was built on the downhill side (Fig. 6). If you find this situation, check carefully for weak footing and cracks in the side foundation, for the fill material often settles and slips, leaving the house suspended, on the verge of tipping downhill, or already settled somewhat and waiting for a heavy winter rain to soften the soil some more.

"Oh, that? Why, that crack has been that way from the time I bought the house. Hasn't changed a bit in six years. It doesn't worry me." This is a very common remark. It doesn't worry the person making it because he or she is going to sell, or perhaps isn't a worrier in the first place. But neither explanation is assurance that the crack won't enlarge.

It's more difficult to examine the foundation of a house built on a concrete slab. You can't get beneath the floor. You can, however, check from the exterior. Weight distribution is very good initially with a concrete slab, for obviously the floor is spread all over the earth and there are no pressure points. The walls do apply weight on the perimeter because of supporting the roof and perhaps another story, so you might think the slab would crack. But not necessarily if it's built correctly. The perimeter should have a deep concrete footing with steel. This footing is a trench maybe a foot wide and eighteen inches deep (see Fig. 7). Properly built, a concrete slab has the proper footing, six inches of crushed rock, a vapor barrier on top of the rock, then wire mesh embedded in the slab.

Stabilizing cracked foundations is difficult to do properly. One method is to drill holes in the foundation and bolt a heavy piece of steel strapping to it. Another is to bore large holes on a slant, in order to get beneath the foundation, then fill the holes with concrete. In some instances, buttresses are erected. None of these jobs is a weekend do-it-yourself project, except the buttresses, which demand digging, building forms, inserting steel, and pouring concrete. (A *long* weekend, maybe.)

A foundation that has settled seriously and is threatening the entire house can often be corrected. One method is to dig a hole large enough for a person to work in and deep enough to be about two feet beneath the bottom of the concrete. Using a pneumatic driver, a three-inch steel pipe is driven into the earth beneath the foundation until a pressure of at least 20,000 pounds per square inch is reached. The pipe is cut off and a plate welded on the top. From that plate a jack can be used to put pressure on the underside of the foundation. In many cases the house is lifted to the desired level; then the entire hole is filled with concrete, jack and all. When

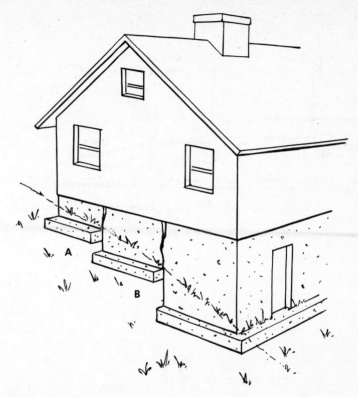

Figure 5
V-Crack Settlement in a Stepped Foundation

the concrete dries, the house is secured to the new foundation.

If you're seriously interested in buying a house with cracks in its foundation, bring in a structural engineer to inspect it. You'll have to pay the inspection fee. If any important problems are discovered, tell the seller and negotiate the cost of repairing them. The structural engineer should be involved in the corrections, verifying that the problems have been fixed in a letter. Keep this letter with the permanent records of the house.

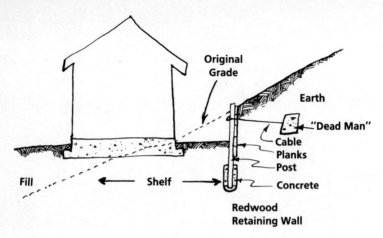

Figure 6
House Built Partly on Fill

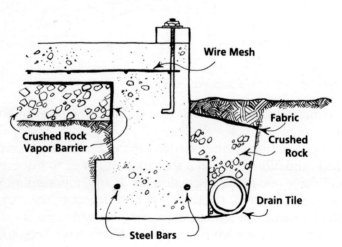

Figure 7
Slab Construction

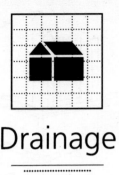

2

Drainage

If you find dampness under the house or evidence of past moisture, it's probably caused by a drainage problem. A wet crawl space, when dried, leaves alligator-hide patterns in the dirt.

Which is more important—good drainage or a good foundation? Both, if possible. What good is a foundation if it rests on poorly drained earth? For this reason good drainage is the most important part of any house. Consider water softening the soil beneath a foundation; the result is mud, softness, and settling. If the house is built on a hillside, a slight slope, lowlands, or a flat area, there are several indicators in the basement (if there is one) that will tell you if drainage is poor.

If all houses could be inspected in the rainy season, you wouldn't need a chapter on drainage, nor would you have to crawl on your stomach beneath the house to do any investigation; you could shine your flashlight to look for dampness. But, alas, it isn't that easy to do a good job. If the earth shows a little moisture but it dries during dry weather, there's no danger to your foundation. However, if ventilation is poor, fungus can start growing, and you have wood rot. Mold growing on the wood is evidence of this. If there is mold, the ventilation may have to be increased. Often there is poor air

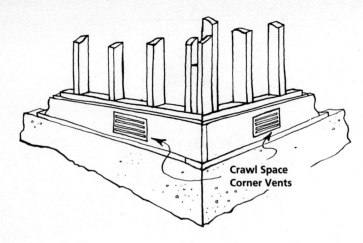

Figure 8
Corner Ventilation

circulation in a corner, so a screened hole or two can be made in that area (Fig. 8). Proper ventilation prevents mold. How much is proper depends upon the moisture condition— ordinarily about two square feet of opening for every twenty-five lineal feet. Contact the local building department for guidelines.

In the summer look for signs of dampness on earth that has dried. If there have been heavy amounts, there will be cracks in the earth. Picture how mud looks when allowed to dry. Deep cracks indicate heavy amounts of moisture. If dried areas have that alligator-hide pattern, look for mold on the wood also. In conditions of poor drainage, houses that have concrete piers supporting the floor may have unlevel floors. The piers have a small area of weight distribution, and they sink into the softened earth. This causes other stress points to bear additional weight, and soon the house has lost stability. It will take new piers and some jacking up to correct this condition.

If there are concrete walls beneath the house, with a concrete floor, and the area is used for a storage room, garage, or game room, you've got to be more observant about drainage. Concrete is not waterproof. If there are boxes stored next to the wall, try to move them, then get your nose in and smell for mustiness; look at the bottoms of the boxes for places where water has dried. Look for stained areas on the concrete. When moisture has evaporated, it leaves a yellowish-brown marking. Frequently you see flimsy white fuzz growing on concrete walls. This is a hydrate, called efflorescence, caused by moisture mixing with acids in concrete. It does no harm, but it does indicate moisture behind the wall. If it's slight, don't worry, but if it's general and heavy, beware of worse conditions, such as a wet basement.

Making concrete walls waterproof is difficult, but there are some good products that claim to do the job. Remember, it's best to prevent the water from striking the wall, but if that can't be done, look into products such as Drylok, Zypex, Thoroseal, RPM, and similar substances.

When you find evidence of much water beneath a house or in a basement, you should first consider whether drain tile can be installed to prevent it. But get prices on the job from two or three professionals before you sign final papers, for you may want to change your offering price.

Installation

Installing drainage isn't all that difficult. Figures 9 and 10 will help you understand the concept of drainage. The first shows a hillside condition. Much of the rainwater striking the earth above the house sinks into the soil and gravitates downhill. When it reaches the concrete wall, it is momentarily stopped; but as more and more water builds up, hydrostatic pressure increases. Since concrete is not waterproof,

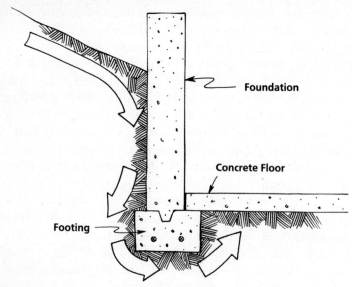

Figure 9
Top Soil

moisture is pushed through, and you have a wet basement. Sometimes you have a concrete foundation that is pushed out of shape by the pressure. The crack between the floor and the wall is a weak place that allows much water to pass. If the earth beneath the floor is dense, not allowing water to percolate into it, then more pressures build up and moisture is forced right up through the concrete floor. You've got to relieve that pressure, or not allow it to form. If there's a continuous concrete foundation all around the house, water builds up on the inside of the bottom foundation and makes a lake, sinking into the soil, softening the earth. In addition, this moisture is unpleasant and conducive to fungus.

The ditch is dug on the exterior of the foundation (Fig. 10). As you can see, the deeper the tile, the more protection. A slight slope should be left on the bottom of the ditch. The

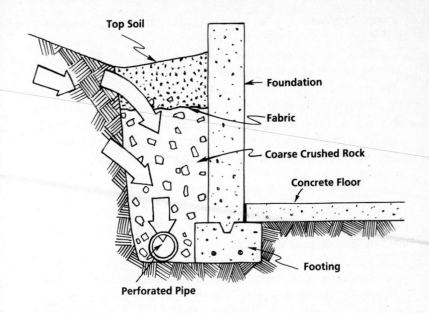

Figure 10
Perforated Pipe

highest point could be in the middle of the back or uphill wall, with the trench sloping slightly to either direction and carried well past the house and down the sides. In older houses drain tile may have been laid on the bottom of the trench. Now plastic perforated pipe is usually used; remember that the holes should be placed down. Then crushed rock, 1½-inch diameter, covers the perforated pipe at least a foot, more if you wish. It's best to coat the wall with hot tar before dumping the crushed rock.

The theory is this: as water reaches the crushed rock, it cannot travel horizontally through it because of the large spaces between the stones. The water trickles down the stones, reaches the perforated pipe, and follows the path of weakest resistance. That is all there is to it. Every situation is different, but the theory is the same.

If there's a concrete patio alongside the back wall, chances are the concrete next to the house will have to be broken up and removed. However, successful drainage sometimes can be attained by digging the trench eight feet from the house at the edge of the patio, especially if there is a good slope to the concrete that carries surface water away from the house. If there's a three-foot walkway, drainage can be placed outside of that.

You can see that the deeper you lay the perforated pipe, the more protection you have. If the wall is eight feet deep, you might get by with going down halfway, but don't depend on it. The theory tells you why.

If you haven't got time to install proper drain perforated pipe before winter, cut interceptor drains in the hillside above the house. These are surface ditches, cut on an angle, that will collect a tremendous amount of water and carry it away before it seeps into the earth. You may be lucky and find they do the job.

Roofs with no gutters spill a great amount of water onto the earth. Sometimes a drainage problem has been solved by adding gutters on the uphill side of the house to collect all the water that would run off the roof and seep into the earth.

If your neighbors have had similar drainage problems, ask how they handled them. They may be able to refer you to competent contractors.

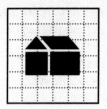

3

Exterior: Paint and Appearance

....

First stand back about twenty feet and eyeball the house from all angles. Line up a wall. You can tell if the house is twisted or leaning a little. Sight down a wall from top to bottom and end to end. The corners should line up. If they are way off, make a note and look for the cause when you get closer. It could be settling in one corner from termites, dry rot, or a poor foundation, or maybe the house has tipped slightly because it has no diagonal bracing. If the corners are just slightly off, forget it. It could have been built that way. Some are. Or maybe you're looking at a loose corner molding. It happens. Craftsmanship suffers when a contractor wants things done in a hurry. Remember, very few houses are absolutely plumb and level.

Paint

Now step up to the house and look carefully at the exterior paint. There are three basic points to note about paint: (1)

peeling and/or blistering, which are nearly always caused by the same problem, (2) checking, (3) chalking or powdering.

Peeling and Blistering

Peeling and blistering occur when moisture is trapped beneath the film of paint. The moisture usually comes through cracks between boards or moldings on the outside of the house, and once in the wall, it wants out. It doesn't all go out the way it came in, so it pushes through the wood and blisters the film of paint. When the blisters get large enough, they split and peeling occurs. Sometimes the moisture is created inside the house. Too much humidity and not enough ventilation is the explanation for that. This is a common problem in snowy areas where winters are long. The house walls are poorly insulated, and too much heat escapes through the walls. As the warm air meets the cold air coming in through the exterior wall, the warm air reaches its dew point and condensation forms. This occurs on the inside of the exterior skin, or sheathing (Fig. 11). If severe enough, it soaks into the wood. Wet wood will not hold paint. If you see peeling and/or blisters of paint, ask when the house was last painted. Paint should stand up four to seven years, depending upon the quality of the paint and the exposure to sunshine. If blisters show on a recently painted house, the cause is undoubtedly moisture forming inside the wall. Later, when you get inside the house, you'll take special care to determine the thickness of the inside wall and whether or not there is insulation in the wall. (More on this later.) Sometimes the seller will say, "I got hold of a poor-quality paint, and that's what made it blister." It could be true but is not generally so. The seller may honestly believe the blisters are caused by the paint. (He or she doesn't know about condensation within a wall.) A whole wall of blistering paint is cause for alarm; an occasional blister is not.

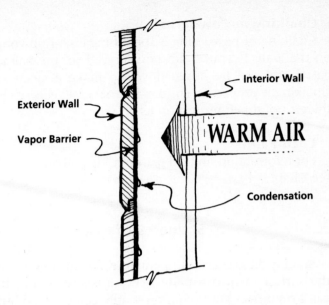

Figure 11
Dew Point

Checking

Checking, a maze of tiny cracks, is usually caused either by insufficient drying time between coats or poor-quality paint. To correct both checking and blistering, sanding, priming, and repainting are necessary. Sometimes you'll find paint over old checking. A sloppy job, really. It looks like alligator hide. A first-class paint job requires removal of all the old paint down to the wood—a big job. There are various methods, depending upon how extensive the old paint is: using a hot iron tool made for the purpose, sanding and scraping, using paint remover, or sandblasting. The last is not a do-it-yourself project.

Chalking or Powdering

Chalking or powdering is something else. Rub your hand on the wall. Is your palm powdery? If so, the paint is oil-based and can be hosed down to make a clean surface. Chalking is proper. Of course, after several years of chalking there's not much protection left.

Lead Paint

For information on lead paint, inside and outside a house, see Chapter 14.

Stained Surfaces

Stain is different. Stain penetrates, paint makes a film on the surface. You can paint over almost all stains, but you can't stain over paint. Stain not only colors wood but lubricates it and keeps it from cracking. Sunshine will dry it out in time. Look closely. If the stain has faded, or if you see several hairline cracks in the wood, the oils have dried out and the stain has lost its power of protection.

Whether they are painted or stained, don't expect all walls to be exactly alike. Sun, wind, and rain act differently on each wall. Sunshine is the enemy of paint, stain, and wood. The more sunshine, the more wear.

Stucco

Is the wall stucco? Most stucco walls have permanent color in the final coat. They don't need paint but will take it if you wish. Scratch the wall and see. The color should be as deep as the scratch. If not, it's been painted. Or find out if the owner knows. Of course, if it's powdered or peeling, you know it's paint.

A few words about stucco. It's an honest product that warns you of the slightest fault. Look carefully at stucco for cracks. Small ones are potential trouble. If moisture gets in, it can swell the wood and push the stucco away from the wall. But worse, a fungus ensues, and dry rot to the wood is the result. Enough dry rot and there's nothing for nails to hold on to and the stucco will fall off.

Where you find cracks that have unlevel edges—that is, one side has pulled away from the wall more than the other—you have what is called a differential separation. For some reason there is poor adhesion to the wall sheathing. It may be that the wire beneath the stucco has broken loose. Perhaps dry rot is the cause. But frequently differential separation is caused by a shift in the earth under the foundation, which has caused a board or two to work loose. Look for a settled foundation under one corner.

Brick

If the exterior is brick, you can quickly learn if the walls are solid brick or veneer. A solid brick wall must have bond beams, or a header course every five or six courses. Headers are bricks turned to expose their ends, or running crosswise to the wall (Fig. 12). Look carefully and you can see the headers (narrow bricks). If the wall is veneer bricks, no headers are required. Instead there are metal ties attached to the wooden wall, extending between courses of bricks. If moisture has seeped through the bricks, dry rot could loosen the ties. See that the bricks are flat against the wall.

**Header Course
or Bond Beam**

Figure 12
Header Course in Brick Wall

Windows and Trim

Other exterior surfaces to inspect are windows. The trim may be freshly painted, but check the condition of the wood next to the glass. Frequently putty dries and shrinks, then pulls away from the glass, breaking the seal. Moisture enters the crack, where it remains without air and starts a fungus, and then dry rot occurs (Fig. 13). Look closely for this. Test the wood with your screwdriver. Is it spongy? soft? If so, dry rot is present.

Dry Rot/Wood Rot

Dry rot is a misnomer. It's plainly wood rot. Wood rot occurs when wood gets wet and cannot dry out with the circulation of air. A fungus starts and feeds on the wood, leaving it weak and useless. You'll find it between boards, especially decks, between stucco and wood, or in wood in the earth, any place where there is a little moisture and no circulation of air. But if you can let air in and stop the moisture, the fungus will die. Any repairs necessary will depend on the extent of the damage.

Those buying or owning a house in areas where winters are cold must check carefully for storm windows. If the house has sealed double-pane windows, you're in luck; they offer good insulation. But if you detect a discoloration between the

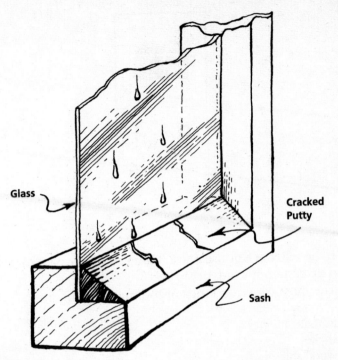

Figure 13
Window Moisture

panes, chances are the seal has been broken and much insulation value has been lost. Such panes are expensive to replace. Homemade storm windows must provide ventilation, or condensation will result. Look for evidence of dried moisture stains.

4

Roof

....

If the seller of a house doesn't brag about the new roof, you can be certain it's old, or suspect.

The most common kinds of roofing material are

asphalt shingles
shakes
wood shingles
tar-and-gravel (also called "built-up" roof)
asphalt-and-fiberglass shingles (these are recent and very
    good)
roll roofing

There are several other good roofing materials, but they are more unusual. A partial list includes

slate
aluminum
tile
terne
asbestos-cement shingles
concrete shingles
plastic shingles

The attic of a house is a good place to start an examination of the roof. Take a strong flashlight with you and find a way up there (usually through a closet).

There's always dust in an attic. If a leak has occurred, the water stain shows when dried. Look, too, for stains on the wood overhead, especially on the ridge where the rafters meet. Now turn off the flashlight and look around. Do you see shafts of light? Let's say it's a wood shingle roof. If it is, you are likely to see light. If you see it only on an angle, don't get alarmed; but if you see it directly overhead, you should put a piece of paper through the holes. Then when you get on the roof you can see what is causing the holes. If the shingles have worn thin or are completely worn out, you're in trouble, for the sun has probably burned right through the wood. If it's going to take a whole notebook of paper to mark all the holes, forget it. You need a new roof. Yet it is surprising how often you can find small holes directly overhead and no indication of leaks. We do know that wood swells when wet. This will seal many small holes, but a responsible home inspector reporting the condition of the roof can't be so optimistic. If the holes were caused by sun-worn shingles that have been burned right through, chances are that almost all the shingles are thin and won't last long.

If it's a composition asphalt shingle roof and you see holes, remember that no swelling is going to occur to help you. Plan to replace the roof covering.

Finally, go back outside and look at the other houses in the neighborhood. If a nearby house built at the same time as the one that you're inspecting has a new roof, you can expect to replace yours soon as well.

Shake Roofs

Many homeowners believe that a shake roof lasts forever. Maybe so, but only in cases where the owners have an unusual idea of eternity. It's true that a shake is a thick, durable piece of wood, but it's still subject to wear. A hand-split, top-grade, no. 1 quality redwood or cedar shake roof with a five-inch pitch will last twenty to twenty-five years in areas where there's strong sunshine six months a year, longer in others. Hand-split shakes will last longer than milled or manufactured shakes. Shakes often get wood rot, but it takes about twenty years. From the ground the shake looks as thick as ever, but "don't go by appearance." If you get on the roof, you may find the wood crumbles beneath your feet. In milling, the fibers are sawn through, disturbing the cell structure of the wood, whereas split shakes break with the grain, and this does not upset the wood fibers. In a hand-split, resawn shake, the split side is exposed to the weather, while the sawn side is smooth and lies flat to the roof.

Wood Shingle Roofs

All shingles are milled, generally from cedar. Shingles have to breathe; that's why you don't find tar paper beneath them, or shouldn't. You can apply composition shingles over wood shingles, but never wood over composition. It's true that the wood shingles beneath the composition can't breathe, but they're no good anyway or you wouldn't be putting a new roof over them.

What you want to look for on a wood shingle roof is how much it has worn. If it has grown thin, it is suspect, for it is brittle and weak and a strong wind will snap it off.

Shingles are not hand-split, and they are thinner than

shakes, so they will not last as long as their thick cousins, the shakes. But the top-grade will last seventeen to twenty-two years in sunny areas, and longer in climates where summers are shorter. It's not unusual to see shingles worn so thin that only threads of wood are left. ''Lacy and leaky,'' roofers say with glee. But before they become that ''pretty,'' they are thin and brittle. You need a new roof.

Before putting up new wood shingles, ask your local building inspector if you need a reroofing permit. Check with your fire insurance company: in some areas the insurance rate is much higher for houses with wood shingle roofs. After the huge 1991 fire in the Oakland, California, hills, some municipalities might even ban wood roofs. There are many roofing materials that resist fire better than wood.

Is there thick moss on the roof? At the start of the rainy season spread lime on the ridges. The water will wash it down and loosen the moss.

A word about that culprit, sunshine. If you could shade your roof, any roof, it would come as close to lasting forever as anything exposed to the air could. It's sunshine that destroys roofs. Look at any roof and you'll find the sides that get less intense sunshine, the east or north, are in better condition than those on the south or west, unless the south and west sides have been reroofed. When a shake or shingle has worn thin or completely through, roofers refer to it as sunburned. It takes several years to wear that much, but it will happen eventually. The length of time depends upon the quality of materials and the intensity of the sunshine. Sapwood (the wood nearer the bark) wears quickly; heart lasts much longer. That ought to tell you to use top-grade, no. 1 shingles or shakes, for they are not made from sapwood.

Asphalt Shingle Roofs

The most common roofing material is asphalt shingles. The typical ones come in many grades and colors. They go by weight, which is a measure not of their thickness but of the quality of material in them. They can be dense and heavy, which is quality without thickness. Roll roofing with a colored mineral surface weighs 90 pounds per 100 square feet. Asphalt shingles weigh anywhere from 200 to 310 pounds per 100 square feet. In the trade this area—100 square feet of roofing material—is called a square. Roofing manufacturers used to have the souls of fishermen—the bigger the better—but they are getting away from the practice of labeling shingles by weight. However, if you ask a few questions, the nominal weight can be learned. A good weight is 265 pounds. Properly applied, a roof of this quality will last fifteen years in the sunny areas of the South and Southwest and longer in the northern states.

The exception to the weight advantage is the new asphalt-and-fiberglass shingle. Because of the materials used, it is thin and light but very durable. Its life expectancy is twenty to twenty-five years in hot climates. Remember that sunshine doesn't discriminate: it destroys all roofs and smiles while doing it. When new, composition shingles have a mineral coating embedded in the surface. If most of the surface is black, with only edges of the colored crystals still intact, you can be certain the roof is in poor condition. When the sun has worked on the composition enough to dry it out completely, there's nothing left to hold the crystals, so they fall off. You need a new roof.

Test a shingle carefully by bending the edge slightly. Did it bend or break off? Pinch off a little. If it crumbles between your fingers, you can be sure there's nothing left to turn away water. When it is lifeless and brittle, it has lost all its oils and has become a sponge. It will break off in a strong wind. The edge you broke off should show a real black substance, not grayish black. A good shingle should give with pressure from your fingernail. If it does, it still has life.

Another area to inspect, without getting on a ladder, is the ends of downspouts. If you see a lot of mineral crystals, it's a good sign that the roof is old and worn.

Tar-and-Gravel Roofs

A tar-and-gravel roof acts in much the same way. The sunshine draws life out of the built-up layers of asphalt paper and tar, and without the asphalt there's nothing left but fibers, which don't turn away water. Look for black spots where the gravel has blown away. If you see a layer or two of split and curled paper, remember it took several years to do that, and several years of sunshine have been working on the entire roof. Beneath that gravel you can be sure the paper has lost much of its life. Also, look around the edges where the nosing (a metal strip) is installed. If the roof is old, it has shrunk and usually is pulled away from the metal. On roofs with a parapet (turned-up edge), the sun wear will be more pronounced on the east and north edge. Check carefully for cracks where the edge turns up. Many tar-and-gravel roofs are flat with a six-inch edge all around. A sprinkler system allows standing water all summer—a good idea since water preserves the roof.

The first and most important point one must learn in evaluating a roof is its age. Ask the owner. If it's a nearly new roof, and you buy the house, ask for the guarantee that came with it. The seller won't need it, and you may. At least you'll have the name of the company that did the job.

If it's an asphalt shingle roof, you can see if there are two or more layers of roofing, but you can't tell if a tar-and-gravel roof has been reroofed. If the house is twenty to twenty-five years old, it better have the second roof. A fifteen- to twenty-year-old roof is suspect, especially if it is not a heavy roof. Again, quality pays off. One can buy a three-, four-, or five-layer roof. Hot tar has been applied between each course and because the tar and gravel congeal together, ascertaining the life of a tar-and-gravel roof is not an exact science. So much for generalities. Sometimes a roofer will add a new nosing over the old one. If you find two nosings, you know the roof has been redone. But that doesn't tell you when, so inquire. City hall may have a building permit record. Reroofing tar-and-gravel roofs is common. All loose gravel is swept off, then more layers of roofing paper and hot tar are added. Good adhesion to the old roof is important. If large bubbles occur, it indicates poor adhesion. The bubbles can split. You should have a roofer look at them.

Slate roofs of poor grade crack and fall off because of the action of freezing and thawing.

Composition shingles and tar-and-gravel roofs can have one of the new synthetic materials added to the surface. Generally this is a pure white substance with white stones embedded in it. This covering will insulate against sunshine to make the house much cooler, but more important, by reflecting the sun's rays it will make the roof last 50 percent longer or more. Thermo Roof is one such trade name. In areas where summers are long and hot, applying such a product to the roof is strongly recommended.

Gutters

Gutters are necessary to collect roof water and, if possible, spill it away from the house so it won't create a drainage problem beneath the house. But equally important is the fact that without gutters the roof water is blown against the house, wearing away the paint, seeping into cracks in the wall or around windows, and starting wood rot.

Wood gutters can rot and the joints can separate. If they are separated, repair them with a good caulking compound; it will last for years. Metal gutters rust through and have to be replaced. Use your screwdriver and test the gutters in several places. One of the best wood preservatives is Tree-seal. This product is made primarily for sealing large cuts in trees, but when it is used as a wood preservative, there is nothing better for painting the inside of wood gutters. It preserves, water-proofs, and gives life to old wooden gutters.

The best gutters are plastic—no rust, no paint. They are available in almost any color.

In snow country, ice dams may occur along the eaves, and water will enter the walls of the house. The cause is melting snow above the living areas, which freezes on the colder eave line. One remedy is to increase the insulation in the attic so that heat doesn't escape through the ceiling. Another is to install electric strips of low voltage along the eaves; this melts the snow and prevents ice dams. These strips are available in most building supply stores in snowy areas. You may also see aluminum replacing the lower few courses of shingles. This helps to prevent ice dams.

Along the eave line is a good place to look for wood rot. The first sign is swelling of the wood, often painted over. Press against it with your screwdriver to learn if it is soft.

Look also at the metal flashing around the bottom of the chimney. Rusted flashing is a sign of future problems. Gobs of tar smeared at the base of the chimney or other penetrations through the roof may be evidence of deferred repairs.

Costs to repair or replace roofs vary depending on the quality of the materials used, the ease or difficulty of getting materials to the roof, and the number of valleys, ridges, vents, skylights, etc., which are obstructions and slow down the work. If you find a poor or suspect roof, get firm costs to repair or reroof, including the cost of removing any previous roofs as required by local guidelines. Obtain exact figures for negotiating purposes. (More on this in Chapter 15.) Costs vary for labor and materials in different areas of the United States, so it is impossible to give prices here. Furthermore, tar and asphalt shingles are petroleum products. Their prices change as often as the wind. What you could do is phone one or two qualified roofers and ask the average cost per square (100 square feet) of roof you need. You'll get a ballpark figure, which is something to go on. Then you be the umpire. Remember: in summer you think about your roof; in winter you worry.

5

Interior

....

If the floors are level and the walls are plumb, we won't spend any time underneath the house determining *why* they are. We'll see what the foundation is, but we won't question it unless there is a question.

Doors and Floors

Stand inside the front door. With the door a couple inches from closing, note the distance from the bottom of the door at the knob end to the floor. Now open it wide and note the distance to the floor. Does it scrape the floor? If so, something is out of line. Either the door is not hung properly, the door jamb on the hinge side is not plumb, the floor is unlevel, or, if the distance is not too great, the hinges are loose or incorrectly sized. Close the door. Is the crack even on the top and down the lock side? Or does it reveal a wedge of air? It shouldn't. If it does, it probably means the opening is not square. Open the door and put your level overhead first, then on the two vertical sides. These are the jambs. If the hinge side is not plumb, the door will probably stick at the bottom when closed. If it doesn't, it means the door has been planed off. With the door closed, put the level on the hinge jamb. If it leans slightly toward the room, this will cause the door to scrape the floor, or come close. Just the opposite if it leans out. Now use your steel ball. Test the floor all around the doorway. The floor is often unlevel in this area, but don't worry too much unless it's severe. That area gets more weather changes than Cape Hatteras. Woodwork shrinks and expands; this can work nails loose. Are the floorboards loose from the joints? Bounce on the floor. Rise on your toes and drop suddenly to your heels. You'll jar your teeth loose, but if the boards are loose you'll hear it. They can be renailed. Now step to the middle of the room. Rise on your toes again and come down hard on your heels. Try to see if the floor vibrates and shakes the room and walls. If it does, it means the joists span too much distance without proper support, or perhaps they are too far apart. They are acting like a spring-board. You'll have to look at the joists when you're beneath the floor.

Some definitions. Floor joists are the parallel members laid on edge, to which the floorboards are nailed. (When joists are overhead, they are called ceiling joists.) A girder—also known as a beam—is the heavy piece of lumber on which the floor joists rest. The girders are in between exterior walls and are supported by posts.

If, for example, the floor slopes toward the center of the room, chances are the floor joists are sagging; the span is too long from wall to girder, or the girder is sagging. You can look for the cause when you get below the floor.

Steel-Ball Test

A word on the steel ball. This is an important extension of the eye. It tells you things you can't see. But it must be remembered that, once it starts rolling, momentum will carry it far beyond an incline. Stop it frequently, then release it. Use the steel ball in all rooms. Make notes as to which floors are unlevel. Having a little diagram of the floor plan to refer to helps when you're underneath the floor. The steel ball is useless on wall-to-wall carpet. The level and a long board can be used when floors are carpeted. Frequently floors slope slightly toward an inner wall, especially if the wall is bearing the weight of another floor above. Over the years the weight has caused the joists to sag, or perhaps supports beneath a girder have sunk a little. If you can easily get beneath this area, it is not difficult to add supports to stabilize the problem. Don't be too eager to jack it up to a level position; you can live with it. Leveling houses can cause trouble. Windows crack, doors no longer operate smoothly, plumbing can break, plaster and walls crack. In older houses, the perimeter foundation often settles from years of weight, causing the floors to sag toward the exterior walls. This is a major repair job; if the slope is slight, forget it. If it's extreme, get a contractor's price and opinion before you buy.

Keep in mind also that green lumber is used to build houses. When it dries, it shrinks, sometimes evenly, sometimes not. Once the shrinking has taken place, conditions stabilize. Frequently unlevel floors are not a sign of any structural fault. However, if you find unlevel floors that slope toward one point—a trend, so to speak—then the cause can usually be located. Beneath the floor, look for rotted wood posts, a cracked and separated foundation that causes settling, a sagging girder that has posts too far apart, sagging joists that span too great a distance for the weight, or termites that have weakened the lumber. Often, too, a concrete pier will sink into the earth because of softening of the bedding from poor drainage. If you find any of these conditions, the mystery is solved; you can then see what has to be done to make corrections.

Learning what causes a defect is fine, but if you can't

explain it, you've got a mystery. Don't buy mysteries, especially serious ones. Read a whodunnit instead. Or attend a magician's show. They're the only mysteries you should spend your money on.

Plaster Cracks

As you go from room to room, use your flashlight to inspect the walls and dark corners; look for cracks. Plaster cracks are common. Plaster acts the same way as stucco. It's stiff and brittle and will show the slightest movement. There are many causes: earthquakes, green shrinking lumber, poor diagonal bracing, weak construction, and, of course, foundation settling or wood rot and termites. Large cracks should be checked to see if the plaster is pulling away from the wall. Run your finger over it. If one side is raised, it undoubtedly is pulling away. Try to determine the extent of poor adhesion, for this will tell you how much has to be removed and replastered. Bubbles or raised portions are definitely indications of pulling away. Be careful. If you press too hard against them, you're likely to lose plaster. Ceiling bubbles are potential trouble.

One cause of plaster coming away from a wall is moisture. For years there could have been a slight leak that has eventually caused decay of the lime in the plaster; then the plaster literally loses its grip.

Gypsum Board Cracks

Gypsum board cracks are something else. If there are straight cracks in the gypsum board (also known by the trade name Sheetrock), it is usually at a joint. Poor taping is generally the cause. You'll frequently find cracks on either side of a doorway or window at the top of the opening. These are header cracks. Not very important. The header is the large beam stretching across an opening (Fig. 14). Often it is one piece, a four-by-twelve. They're put up green and swollen with water. When they're nailed, moisture splatters from them with each blow. Carpenters like them. "Just like nailing bananas," they say. But you can imagine the shrinkage that occurs over the next year or so. In the meantime, gypsum board has been nailed to the header and the studs, then taped and painted. The shrinkage will not be uniform. A crack appears in the gypsum board where the header meets the stud on either side. Once the shrinkage has stopped, fill the cracks with spackling paste and repaint.

If the interior walls are Sheetrock and you find a large diagonal crack, you can be certain it was caused by a severe movement, a shifting or settling. Note whether the floor is unlevel near the wall. Check the baseboard; is it firmly touching the floor? It takes a drastic movement to break gypsum board diagonally. Perhaps you'll find the cause beneath the floor. Make a note to look.

Wherever you see cracks in plaster or gypsum board and the edges of the cracks are darkened, it's an indication of moisture—a leak. It may be from an old leak, but find out for sure. Cracks that have clean edges are the result of movement only.

The interior walls may also have a glazed appearance, caused by heavy tobacco smoke. Removing this layer is a messy job that will add to the cost of repainting the walls.

Testing for Insulation

In two or three rooms, remove the plate from an electric outlet on the exterior walls only. Be sure to check that all exposed wires are connected before wedging a bamboo

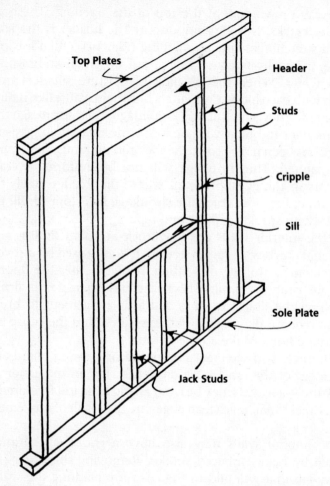

Top Plates

Header

Studs

Cripple

Sill

Sole Plate

Jack Studs

Figure 14
Header Beam

chopstick between the box and the wall covering (Fig. 15). Do *not* attempt this insulation test if any wires are disconnected. Push the chopstick gently through to the exterior wall. Feel for a slight resistance; you're determining whether or not there is insulation in the wall. Move the instrument about a little. Nothing? Okay. Try in a few more rooms. One test is not conclusive. You'll know if you meet a spongy resistance; if so, you've got insulation in that wall. It's good to know, for it tells you of hidden quality. Later you will inspect the attic for insulation.

A note on insulation. Generally, depending upon the type of construction, the heat loss and obverse heat gain in summer through walls is from 15 to 20 percent without insulation. Attics are something else. If you're going to insulate one place only, choose the attic. A 20 to 30 percent heat loss and gain passes through that area. Attics are easy to insulate after the house is built if the access is provided. Insulation can be blown in in a couple of hours, or fiberglass rolls or batts can be laid in. Foil should always face toward the living area. The typical do-it-yourself kind is fiberglass, six to nine inches thick, with foil backing.

Condensation can be a serious problem in cold weather areas. If there is enough condensation forming within a wall, it can run down to the sill plate and start wood rot. When this condition exists, the walls, both on the interior and exterior, first show rotting at the floor level. There is not only severe condensation but serious heat loss in the winter. It's a poorly built house. Once the walls are complete, it's very difficult to do a good job of insulating. The only effective way is to remove either the exterior or interior wall. Sometimes it's worth it. (More on insulation in Chapter 11.)

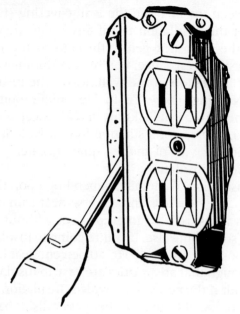

Figure 15
Testing for Insulation

Diagonal Bracing

Diagonal bracing is very important. There should be diagonal bracing in almost all walls, but you can't detect it if the walls are covered. However, if the house is on a hillside, there's generally space beneath the main floor that is not finished. The substructure posts and beams that are exposed offer an excellent opportunity to look for diagonal bracing in the house. If no diagonal bracing exists, it is a minus, but the braces are easy to apply. When the posts are several feet apart, the diagonal braces should be two-by-sixes, and they should be bolted to the posts, rather than nailed (Fig. 16).

Another good method of diagonal bracing is the use of plywood gussets (Fig. 17). Gussets are triangular pieces of

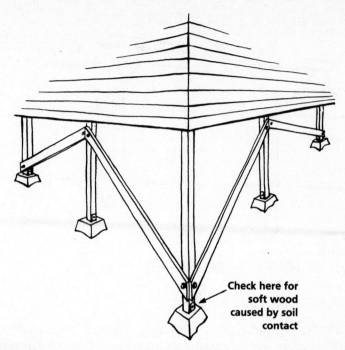

Check here for
soft wood
caused by soil
contact

Figure 16
Diagonals

plywood ⅝-inch thick or more, fastened with numerous nails on both post and beam. They should be a minimum of two feet long. The longer the better. In addition to diagonal strength, gussets offer excellent fastening where posts meet beams. Don't trust toe nails; the only good they do is to hold the post to the beam. The use of gussets and/or diagonal braces could mean the difference between saving or losing a house during an earthquake.

A point to remember: sheets of plywood nailed to exposed studs or posts offer excellent diagonal bracing and act as a finish material at the same time.

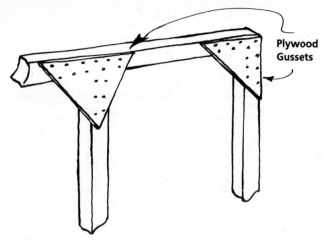

Figure 17
Using Plywood Gussets for Diagonal Bracing

The Attic

All attics should have ventilation, whether improved or not. If unimproved, they're easy to ignore, but they're not ignoring you. During the summer a tremendous amount of heat can accumulate in that space, and without ventilation it can't escape. This is why houses stay warm so long into the night. A properly ventilated house has screened or louvered holes either in the soffits or between the rafters where the wall meets the roof, and up near the ridge line. This allows through ventilation. As hot air escapes through ridge vents, it draws cooler air through the lower vents. In the summer it can lower house temperatures ten to twenty degrees. If there are no vents along the eave line, you can still have them up at the ridge and they will help somewhat. How much ventilation should a house have? There are so many conflicting figures that it would be difficult to give any here. Check the building codes in your area. But first use your head. If there aren't any vents, there should be. Whatever you add is more than you had.

There are excellent rotor-type ventilators for roofs. They have no motor, but as heat escapes it revolves the finned vent; the more it revolves, the more heat it expels. In some cases a fan is required to do the job.

Note: Attic ventilators should remain open summer and winter. Summer ventilation lowers the attic temperature and cuts down on air-conditioning costs. Winter ventilation removes moisture that could condense in the attic space and start dry rot. In the northern states look for dry rot near the eave line in attics.

Structural Lumber

While in the attic you have an opportunity to inspect structural lumber and methods of building. Look at the size lumber used for rafters and their distance apart. If the lumber used is rough or unsurfaced, it is full-dimensional and stronger than smoothed or surfaced lumber. On a steep roof in snowy states the rafters should be two-by-six, sixteen inches apart, and have knee-wall bracing to support heavy snow loads (Fig. 18). Check on rafter sizes by consulting the local building official. The steeper the roof, the less vertical load the rafters carry. Check also the fastening method where knee walls and collar beams meet the rafters. If they are bolted together or have plywood or metal gussets, they are better than nails. That's care and quality. Also, you should stand back from the house and sight the roof. If the ridge is sagging like an old horse's back, beware. Look at the rafters. If they are sagging from the ridge to the eave line, they're too small for the distance they span. They won't straighten up. Bracing can be added to hold them, but it's a poor situation if they dip. Incidentally, a pair of binoculars can be used successfully to examine the condition of a roof, and they are much safer than ladders.

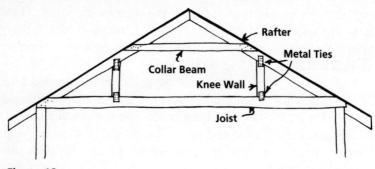

Figure 18
Roof Rafters

"Can I build a room in this attic?" is a common question. Doing so often requires more than laying down floorboards. Those ceiling joists inviting plywood and carpets are not made to hold much more weight than the ceiling. If you start walking on them, they'll sag. In all probability new joists will have to be "sistered" alongside the existing ones. The new ones will be larger and extend above the old ones, so the weight will bear on them, leaving the old ones holding the ceiling. This is a job that requires experience and know-how if anyone occupying the attic hopes to stay up there.

In the southern states the roof should have hurricane ties holding the roof securely to the walls. Look for them in the attic. They may be metal strips, angle irons, plywood, or wood.

6

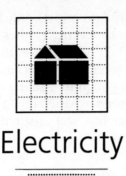

Electricity

························

For most people electrical wiring holds more mystery than any other aspect of a house, and it should. *Respect electricity.* Nevertheless, with a little basic knowledge it is easy to examine and test the electrical system.

In buying a house, you will want to reassure yourself on two points about the wiring: that there aren't any ominous signs of poor work, and that the system has enough power for all your appliances. Inspecting the electrical system starts at the service panel, which you might know better as the circuit-breaker panel or fuse box, and moves to the wiring and outlets.

Wires that conduct electricity come in a variety of sizes and capacities, starting with the large, thick, black wires originating from the power pole. These conductors carry a large amount of power to the service panel, usually located near the electric meter. Thinner wires carry electricity from the service panel to outlets throughout the house. A circuit breaker or fuse is installed in each circuit to ensure that it does not become overloaded with current, which might cause overheating and a fire.

Count the conductors leading from the pole outside the house to the service panel. If there are no more than two conductors, you may find outlets only for light fixtures and small appliances. Your electric clothes dryer, water heater, stove, or table saw will not function in a house served by a two-wire overhead service-drop because it will not have the 220-volt circuits they require. Adding more circuits will require changing the service panel. If you count three conductors, you can probably feel assured that large electric appliances will work.

A few houses are served by underground service-lateral conductors, so you won't see the wires overhead. Underground conductors are fairly new, so these houses are almost certain to be wired sufficiently for clothes dryers and other large appliances.

The Service Panel

The service panel distributes electricity in protected circuits. Hazards don't exist in a properly maintained service panel. Problems arise when the service panel has been modified by unqualified people. The seller might have had the right idea when adding a circuit for the spa, for instance, but forgot to ground the spa wiring.

Let's take a closer look at potential trouble spots in the service panel. Read the capacity of the panel from the label pasted on its door. A 60-amp service panel is barely adequate; plug in a hair dryer and watch the lamps flicker! It would be wise to invest in a 100-amp system. Large homes should have a 200-amp panel to accommodate heavy loads, like an additional living unit or a well-equipped workroom. Such a panel allows twelve to twenty-four circuits, which is excellent power distribution. Some local ordinances require all new homes to have at least a 200-amp service panel. The extra cost of upgrading a service panel is small and is borne by the homeowner after purchase.

Open the service panel. Inside you will see either fuses or circuit breakers (see Figs. 19 and 20 for simplified drawings of service panels.) Fuses are fine if they are properly sized, but it's easy to mix them up. The use of improper fuses can be avoided by installing tamper-proof fuses of the correct amperage, known as S-type fuses. Beware of a penny replacing a fuse!

Circuit breakers provide a safe way to protect wiring and are always labeled with their amperage ratings. If a fuse shorts out because its circuit is overloaded, it must be replaced, but a circuit breaker can simply be switched back on after the cause of the short is removed. Since circuit breakers have moving parts, moisture and dust can make them freeze up. Circuit breakers in exposed locations should be manually tripped twice a year—one way to remember is to trip the switches on the Saturday when you must reset your clocks anyway for daylight saving time.

Are the circuits properly identified? Labels are very helpful for repairs and when you sell the house. Do you see any extra burned-out fuses? These may be evidence of overloaded circuits. Are there any openings in the panel? A service panel with unused openings is hazardous because curious fingers or a misplaced tool might accidentally meet the current. Is the panel securely fastened to the wall?

You may find aluminum wiring in the service panel. Less expensive than copper, aluminum wire was used mainly for service entrance conductors and for circuits supplying large appliances like clothes dryers and stoves. It has a tendency to loosen the screws that hold it to the terminals. These loose connections force the electricity to arc across space, and that can cause fires. Still, very few problems have occurred because of aluminum conductors. The connections should be checked once a year, or you can ask an electrician to apply an oxide inhibitor to the connections to prevent arcing for several years.

The service panel may be grounded with a copper wire

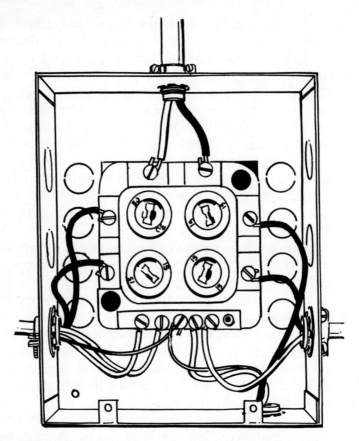

Figure 19
A Fuse Box

about as thick as a chopstick running from the service panel to a buried rod or pipe. This ground wire must be securely attached to a metal block inside the panel, along with any other bare conductors. If you don't find a ground wire like this, talk with the owner about installing a properly grounded service panel. Almost all home electrical systems need grounding.

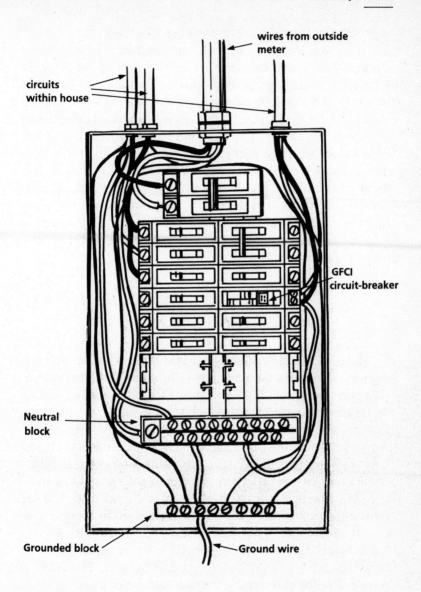

Figure 20
A Grounded Circuit-Breaker Box

Finally, subpanels are sometimes installed "down line" from the service panel to distribute and protect additional circuits. Like a service panel, a subpanel must be properly secured to the house, have no unused openings, and contain properly identified fuses or circuit breakers. The subpanels should be located in accessible areas. Subpanels located in closets should be kept clear of combustibles like clothing and boxes. Look for extra burned-out fuses. If you find more than one subpanel, the house may have a poorly planned electrical distribution system that should be checked by a licensed electrical contractor. Corrective measures may include installing a larger main service panel. If electrical hazards are detected, the cost of installing a larger service panel is the seller's responsibility.

Service-Panel Connections

Inside the main service panel you'll see a variety of conductors. Generally speaking, you should find all the neutrals (wires wrapped in white insulation) securely attached to one metal block. There must be a chopstick-sized wire between that neutral block and the grounded block described above. Any bare wires must be attached to the grounded block and may also be in contact with the neutral block. The "hot" conductors (wires wrapped in colored insulation) are individually attached to each fuse or circuit breaker. If you see more than one colored conductor connected to a single fuse or circuit breaker, you have discovered hazardous wiring. Each black, red, or other colored wire must be properly protected with its own fuse or circuit breaker. The seller is responsible for eliminating hazardous overloads.

Inside the service panel everything should look neat and tidy. If the wires are tangled like spaghetti in a colander, you may have problems. If the wires look as neat as a package of dry spaghetti, you are probably looking at a well-maintained service panel.

Most houses will contain only three sizes of copper conductors: #14, #12, and, in a few places, #10. You may be lucky enough to find these numbers printed on the wires' insulation, but it's better to familiarize yourself with conductors at the local hardware store. Get a short piece of each. Peel off an inch of the insulation to see the difference between the three sizes: the smaller the number rating, the thicker the copper, and the more electricity it can safely conduct. Take a sample of #14, lay it across your first and second fingers, and press it with your thumb. Now do the same with the #12. The #14 bends more easily, doesn't it? Now you have two tests: sight and feel.

The size of a fuse or circuit breaker must match the size of the wire circuit connected to it. If the fuse or circuit breaker is oversized, the circuit can overheat before burning out a fuse or tripping the circuit breaker. If you find an overfused circuit in the service panel, you should really think twice about the house. A seller should never show a house with overfused circuits!

Compare the fuses or circuit breakers in the service panel with the conductors connected to them. Here is the maximum amperage rating of a fuse or circuit breaker that can be used with each common type of conductor:

Wire Size	Fuse/Circuit Breaker
#14	15 amps
#12	20 amps
#10	30 amps

If you find the circuits underfused, you're safe but could be inconvenienced. For example, a #12 conductor connected to a 15-amp fuse won't overheat, but you couldn't draw as much power from that circuit as a 20-amp fuse would safely allow. A hair dryer pulling 16 amps would blow out a 15-amp fuse even though the #12 conductor can transmit that much electricity safely. Ask the seller to establish the correct sizes of fuses, mark the panel accordingly, and provide an adequate supply of replacement fuses.

You may also find 30-, 40-, or 50-amp fuses and circuit breakers. If properly wired, these should be attached to unusually large conductors (with wire sizes below #10). It is rare for appliance circuits of these sizes to be improperly wired because they have usually been installed by licensed electricians.

Wiring Throughout the House

Start your wiring inspection above the service panel. Check the underfloor and in the attic if you can. Typical house wiring systems consist of plastic sheathed cable or a variety called knob-and-tube. Either type of wiring works fine if it's intact. Sheathed cable is cylindrical, about ½ inch in diameter. Sheathing may be white, gray, or black. Knob-and-tube wiring can be found in older houses. It consists of individually insulated strands of wire threaded through porcelain tubes between wood-framed walls and ceilings.

Like the service-panel wiring, the house wiring will probably be fine if it was installed by an electrical contractor and left alone. Problems arise when do-it-yourselfers add new circuits, light fixtures, or receptacles. Look at all the wiring to determine what was originally installed. The areas above and below the kitchen and garage are the most likely places to find additions. All of the original conductors will be covered with sheathing of the same vintage. If some sheathed conductors look newer than others, you are probably looking at new electrical work that would have required a permit and documented inspections.

Ask the seller to show you a permit to verify that any additional wiring was inspected and approved by the local building department. If no permit is available, ask the seller to have any additions approved by taking out an electrical permit now and having the work inspected. The cost of legalizing electrical work done without a permit should be absorbed by the seller.

Electrical Outlets

Older houses usually have fewer light fixtures and outlets. Explore each room to determine if you're satisfied with the number and location of the light fixtures. If your last home had lights installed in the ceiling and this one doesn't, you'll have to buy floor and table lamps. Look at the electrical outlets. Are there enough? Properly spaced receptacles will reduce the number of extension cords squeezed through doorways, strung between windows, and placed under carpets, producing a safer and more attractive home.

Ask the seller to open up a few of the permanent light fixtures. Check the conductors leading to them. Is the insulation brittle? If so, the fixtures may have been overheated. Damaged or poorly insulated wiring is hazardous and should be replaced at the seller's expense.

In the kitchen, observe the lights as the refrigerator cycles on and off and as you turn the electric stove on and off. Too many light fixtures or receptacles on the same circuit as a large appliance may cause the lights to flicker. When people were adding garbage disposals to their kitchens, some took the shortcut of installing the disposal on the same circuit as the lights. This becomes obvious if the lights dim when you turn on the disposal. Loose connections can also cause flickering. Flickering light fixtures should be checked and repaired by a qualified electrician at the seller's expense.

You may find outlets wired with aluminum conductors. In order to verify that such an outlet was properly chosen, *shut off the power*, make sure there's no electricity flowing through the outlet, and unscrew it from the wall or ceiling. Inspect the area where the aluminum conductor is connected to the outlet. You should see the letters CO/ALR or CU/AL on the terminals or on the back of the outlet. If the outlet is not labeled in this way, it should be replaced. The seller is responsible for such work.

Grounded Electrical Outlets

If the service panel is grounded, check all the circuits in the house to make sure they are properly grounded, too. Older wall receptacles are identified by two parallel slots for two-pronged plugs; newer grounded receptacles have a third, U-shaped opening below. Properly wired three-holed outlets are safer than the two-holed ones because, if an appliance develops a short, the current will travel through the ground wire rather than through you!

Inspect three-holed outlets carefully. Each must have a third bare wire connected to a green screw on the receptacle in order to be properly grounded. Frequently a do-it-yourselfer will substitute the three-pronged receptacle but forget, or be unable, to attach the ground wire to it. This outlet is no safer than the original two-holed affair. It is forbidden by the National Electrical Code to install a three-holed receptacle without the ground wire. Don't be deceived into assuming each outlet is individually grounded. Check them all!

Some local ordinances require that all bathroom outlets be grounded. A call to the local building department will help in determining your local electrical codes. Outlets for larger appliances like clothes washers and dryers should be grounded the same way. Appliances in the garage should all be grounded to water pipes.

Circuit testers are available at most hardware stores for under ten dollars. To test whether a receptacle is grounded, make sure the power is on. Note that one of the parallel slots in the receptacle is smaller than the other. The smaller slot is "hot" and carries the live current to the appliance. Place one end of the tester into the "hot" side, and the other end into the U-shaped slot (Fig. 21). If the receptacle is properly grounded, you will see the tester's bulb light up. If nothing happens, go to the service panel and turn off the circuit. Go back to the receptacle and place one end of the tester into each parallel slot. The test bulb should not light up. If it does, you've shut off the wrong circuit—this is why labeling fuses and circuit breakers is so important. Find the right circuit and shut it off before you open up the receptacle.

Once you have verified that the outlet is not energized, you can safely remove the plate covering it. Underneath the plate, you will find two additional screws. After removing these, you can pull the receptacle out of the wall. If you don't find a bare conductor attached to a green screw on the back of the receptacle, the outlet is not grounded. This is a hazard.

While checking that all receptacles are properly grounded, you should also make sure they are not cross-wired. Simply place one end of the tester into the *larger* slot, and place the other end into the U-shaped hole. If the bulb lights up, the receptacle is cross-wired. It's such a simple test, so why not check all of the receptacles? Outlets that aren't properly grounded or are cross-wired must be corrected by the seller.

Newer houses will have wall receptacles in the kitchen, bathrooms, and garage protected with ground-fault circuit

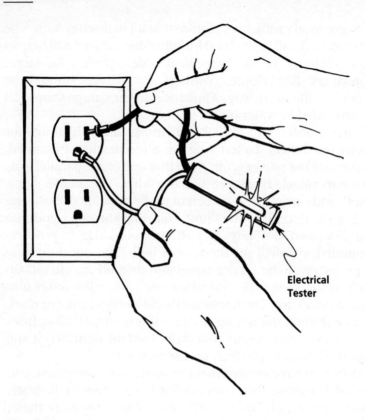

Electrical
Tester

Figure 21
Testing for Ground

interrupters (GFCIs). These outlets have small buttons labeled TEST and RESET. Ask the seller for the manufacturer's
instructions on testing them. Verifying that GFCI-protected
receptacles have been properly installed takes a more sophisticated tool. If you want, ask your hardware dealer for a
ground-fault tester, which costs less than fifty dollars.

Conclusion

If you don't want to inspect a house wiring system in detail, simply keep your eyes open for obvious signs of potential problems: messy service panels, burned-out fuses, extra subpanels, and signs of new (and possibly unprofessional) wiring. Look for flickering lights, and make sure there are enough fixtures and outlets for your needs. If the seller mentions recent electrical improvements, be sure to ask for a "finaled" permit—one with the electrical inspector's signature. All electrical work requires a permit and inspections by local authorities. Finaled permits should be kept with other important house records.

After concluding your inspection of a house's electrical system, discuss any concerns with the seller. If you see problems, you might suggest that the seller share the cost of having a local electrical inspector conduct a thorough inspection. Another good idea would be to have a licensed electrical contractor work together with you and the seller when inspections and repairs are made. Finally, you may want to have a representative of the local utility look over your wiring—this inspection will probably be free! Be aware that sellers do not need to bring the house wiring "up to code" unless a local ordinance requires it.

7

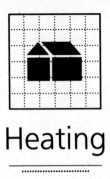

Heating

························

As you walk from room to room, carefully observe the heat registers to determine whether the heating system is the gravity or forced-air kind. If the registers are overhead, the furnace is forced-air. If they are on the floor or near the floor, it could be either. If there aren't any registers, the heat comes from another source. There aren't many systems available, and only a few are widely used. This chapter will look at the most popular ones.

Forced-Air Furnace

Forced-air gas furnaces have a motor that pushes the heated air through ducts, which can run both long and level and up, down, and around obstacles. The unit can be located in the basement, attic, garage, or a closet. They're very adaptable, as you can see, don't take up much room, and are very efficient. In addition to pushing hot air through the ducts, the motor sucks air from inside the house and reheats it. This air is filtered, or should be. Frequently filters are as dense as plywood. A badly maintained filter starves the furnace of air, cuts down on efficiency, and is the most likely cause of a cracked heat exchanger.

The forced-air oil furnace works in the same way as the gas furnace. The main difference is that the oil furnace has a motor in front of the furnace to pump oil.

Gravity Furnace

A gravity furnace has no filter, no motor. The ducts must slope up from the furnace to the registers so the warm air can rise. A gravity furnace is always in the basement. And the gravity furnace does not have high-voltage electric wires running to it. There may be small, low-voltage wires, but they are for the thermostat. Since it has no motor, the gravity furnace is quieter. It is not as quick with the heat, but it has no working parts to break down, and it doesn't blow dust around.

Floor Furnace

A floor furnace is essentially gravity heat, without ducts. The main criticism of it is that distribution is not good, for you have heat in one place and not in each room. The grill gets very hot, creating a hazard for children, but it's great to stand over on a cold morning.

Wall Heaters

Wall heaters, sometimes called panel ray, are common. These are space heaters, and they do heat the space around them adequately but do not distribute it well. As a result, a wall heater in the middle of the house will require that bedroom doors be kept open if sleepers want to stay warm at night. Wall heaters are good for rooms that have been added to a house.

Electric Heat

Electric heat is used a great deal. It's good, clean, quiet, and safe, if wired properly, and has no gases or vents. Installation is generally less expensive than for gas heaters. Intertherm, sometimes called liquid electric, is a perimeter-type heater with a sealed-in liquid that heats grills and convects heat— either 115 volt or 230 volt. Calculate the cubic feet of space in the room; if you figure one watt for each cubic foot of space, you'll be close to the adequate amount of heat using liquid electric.

Hydronic Furnace

Another heating system that is gaining favor is the hydronic furnace. This is forced hot water. Small baseboard radiators are installed and connected to a heating plant and storage tank. Hot water is forced by pump throughout the system. It is very good heat, quiet and clean. In addition, this system can supply hot water instantly to faucets, thus eliminating a water heater. The hot water doesn't come from the boiler but from a coil located inside the boiler, so the water to faucets is hotter than that going to the room heaters.

Radiant Heat

Radiant heat is generally from the floor. Pipes are embedded in concrete or sometimes placed between wood floor joists, and hot water is pumped through them. Occasionally you'll find the pipes in the ceiling. Radiant heat requires a large heater to heat the water, a pump to circulate it, and preferably an expansion tank. Various zones of heat control can be arranged when the system is being installed, but not after the pipes are covered. About the only thing you can check for on radiant heat is the pump and whether or not there's a leak in any pipe. Often a pressure gauge, which would tell you if water is leaking, is installed in the line. If the leak is large enough, water can be heard entering the pipes near the heater. It is virtually impossible to determine where a leak has occurred in pipes embedded in concrete. If they are copper pipes, as they should be, the chance of a leak is slight.

It's not unusual to find electric radiant heat from the floor or from the ceiling. Both are good.

Checking a Furnace

Forced-air furnaces are the most common because of their adaptability—that is, they can be installed in small areas and, as stated, do not require a basement.

The most important part of a furnace is the heat exchanger. Essentially this is a metal box enclosed inside the furnace jacket (see Fig. 22). The hot air accumulates outside the combustion chamber and is blown into the plenum. The plenum is the metal box that collects all the hot air. From the plenum the hot air is dispersed through the various heat ducts to different rooms. A serious fault in a gas furnace is a crack in the heat exchanger, because carbon monoxide would leak through the crack and be blown into the heating ducts (follow the arrows in Fig. 22).

There are four good tests to determine if the heat exchanger is firm. First, close all dampers but one, as close to the plenum as possible, then turn on the main flame. Study it

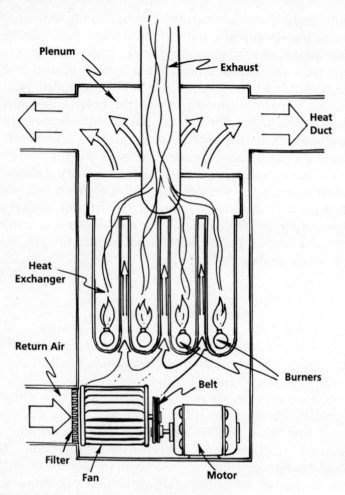

Figure 22
Forced-Air Furnace

carefully to note its color and how it stands up. You can see it through the pilot-light hole. Then take your head away from the hole and turn on the blower. If there is a hole in the exchanger, the flame may be pushed out through the viewing hole. The flame should not change. Second, with dampers open, turn on the main flame and again watch it carefully, then turn on the blower. If the flame boils up vigorously or slants off in any direction, it is probably being sucked toward a hole in the exchanger. Again, the flame should not change. These tests take some experience.

Third, use a small mirror on the end of a stick, secured by a universal joint (check with an automobile parts store). Insert the mirror in the hole above the burners, and with a flashlight you can see an image of the exchanger. Move the mirror around to view as much surface as possible. Frequently you have to unscrew a small plate covering part of the burners to get a better view.

Paint a good amount of oil of wintergreen on the heat exchanger on both sides of each burner. You can use a 1/4-inch long-handled brush bent at a 30-degree angle. Then, if there is a summer switch, turn it on. Check for odor at each heat register. You should not get any. If you do, beware; you undoubtedly have a cracked heat exchanger or pinholes that are difficult to see. If there is no summer switch, you have to turn on the furnace, then wait for the fan. Don't be in too much of a hurry. Allow the odor to accumulate and seek the holes. The flame will quickly burn away the oil on the exchanger, but the odor will have done the job for you.

If you discover a hole, the furnace should probably be replaced. Sometimes the heat exchanger itself can be changed. Don't let anyone weld a hole; in fact, in most states it's against the law. How secure would you feel with a new patch in an old exchanger?

In a gravity furnace it is harder to detect a cracked heat exchanger because there is no blower to suck the air and make the flame boil. If there's a large hole, of course the flame would lean in the direction of the hole. The wintergreen test is very good to use on gravity furnaces. And you should use the mirror to look closely at the heat exchanger. Also, reach in and tap lightly on the metal walls with a small hammer. They should ring, or at least make a hollow sound. If they are cracked badly, you will hear a dead sound. This latter test is not dependable for the novice. Better be sure.

The sure proof of a faulty heat exchanger is actually to see the hole. The boiling flame tests will tell you something is wrong and requires further checking. If you're unsure, you should first ask your utility company to check it. Some do it free. Others have a minimal charge. These companies want good, safe equipment in homes and are very cooperative about such matters. Their recommendations are very reliable. They're not in the business of selling furnaces.

A floor furnace is easy to check. Remove the grill from the floor and get down on your knees and look it over carefully with your flashlight. Look for small holes with a little carbon around them. Tap the exchanger and listen. Turn on the flame and look carefully for pinholes in the metal that would show the flame beneath. Also, the flame should burn steadily and not grow or lean to one side.

If you learn that the furnace or heater is in good condition, check the vent pipe to see if all connections are firm, so that it will carry all exhaust gases to the outside. Look at the burners; are they pitted, corroded, deteriorated? If so, you can be sure it's an old unit. Check the heat ducts. Are they insulated? All joints connected? Sometimes dogs get into the basement and run around, knocking against ducts, tearing the insulation loose, dislodging joints. Does the loose insulation need to be tested for asbestos? Are there dampers in the ducts? This is important, for everyone has different demands for heat in various rooms, and the proper control is near the furnace. It's not the same to cut off heat at the end of a run, for much heat is then wasted coming all the way from the furnace, and most of it is going to leak out.

Another important aspect of any gas furnace is combustion venting: the presence of oxygen to feed the burning gas. Wherever the unit is placed, there must be oxygen coming into the space. It may be through a pipe from the outside; if the unit is in the basement, the area should not be closed tight. This is true for gas water heaters also. If the pilot light goes out frequently, it may be from lack of oxygen.

And, of course, the furnace should always respond to the thermostat. Try it and see. In a forced-air furnace, look at the fan housing. If the filter hasn't been changed frequently, this housing can be very dirty. This is dangerous because it will cause overheating. If the fan is belt-driven, handle the belt and see if it is in good condition. They do get old, then split, crack, and break, usually on Christmas Eve. If the unit is dirty and appears untended, it needs servicing, that is, oiling, cleaning, and adjusting. A fire safety technique is checking the area above the heating unit to make sure there aren't any exposed wooden beams. If there are, cover them with a noncombustible material such as metal or a one-hour, fire-rated ($^5/_8$ type X) gypsum board.

Older Heating Systems

In some old Victorian homes, especially in the eastern states, you are likely to find a steam or gravity hot-water system. In many instances this is a lucky find. These old systems are extremely durable—they're made to last and probably have many years of service in them. There is nothing wrong with them but for two things: (1) from a modern viewpoint they are slow, and (2) many of these older heating systems are insulated with asbestos. Until recently, asbestos was used as an insulator around heating pipes, in heating systems, and in ceiling blocks. When examining an older home's heating system, be sure to look carefully at the heating unit itself. If the unit appears to be covered by a cloth or plasterlike material, you have reason to suspect that the substance is asbestos.

Do not disturb any material that might contain asbestos. This situation requires professional testing (see Chapter 14 for more information).

Whatever the case, you'll probably want a new boiler, and it would pay you to get one. The modern ones are efficient and can save you up to 25 percent in fuel consumption. Also, the new boilers are much smaller than the old, put out more heat, and leave more room in the basement. And with a new boiler you can have instantaneous hot water at any faucet without installing a separate water heater.

If you don't like the old radiators, you can replace them with new ones designed to fit along the baseboards. By adding a pump to the system you can have a hydronic heater. This will give you more uniform heat and quicker response. A few pipes installed at the boiler can do the job. This takes know-how. You should get expert advice.

With forced hot water you can have zone control heating, that is, thermostats installed in several sections of the house to keep some rooms cooler than others.

Judging Heating Capacity

If you wonder whether the furnace is large enough to heat the house adequately, there are many factors to consider. How well is the house built? Is it flimsily constructed, with $1/4$-inch plywood interior walls and $3/8$-inch exterior walls with no insulation? If you have $1/2$-inch gypsum board interior and $3/4$-inch exterior sheathing, the heat loss will be less. But mainly, insulation and what climatic area you live in are the biggest factors. There are other things to consider also: How much glass is there? Is the glass double-pane? Is the house two stories with one furnace?

Even though we live in the United States, heat is still measured by BTUs (British thermal units). For practical purposes, one BTU is the amount of heat given off by burning an old-fashioned wood match. The number of BTUs put out by the furnace is important, but there is no set formula for determining how many BTUs will do the job. In a well-insulated house the number of BTUs required is much lower than heating engineers have demanded in the past.

The BTU capacity of the furnace is plainly marked on a logo plate, usually on the front of the unit. There'll be several figures, but the one you're interested in is the figure after the word "Input."

Another thing to look for is a summer switch. You'll find it only on a forced-air furnace. If there is one, it will be to one side of the front of the furnace and will be marked "Summer Switch" or sometimes "Manual" or "Automatic." It starts only the motor. The purpose, of course, is to circulate air through the ducts. It's not air conditioning, but moving air does offer some relief on a hot day. If you like the idea, the switch can be moved to a more convenient location in the living quarters. And if there isn't a switch, it can be installed.

A word of caution. There are electric wires leading to the furnace, and there should be a switch in the line. It may be on the outside of the furnace or on a wall nearby. It's almost always a regular wall switch, like the ones you have for lights, and serves to cut the electricity while servicing the furnace. It is not the summer switch.

Wood-Burning Heaters

Wood-burning stoves and fireplace inserts offer alternative methods of heating homes in areas where wood is abundant. For your safety, the walls adjacent to the stove as well as the stove's foundation should be made of noncombustible material. Examples of noncombustible materials are millboard, brick, and concrete.

Ask the seller to give you all the records pertaining to the stove: the manufacturer's installation directions, the permit showing it was inspected, and service records. Make sure it was installed and maintained safely. Your life might depend on that.

Install a wood stove if you want; you'll have a new friend if you do. It's great heat. Check around; there are many excellent stoves on the market. Consult *Mother Earth News*. It can give you much information on wood-burning stoves.

A note on these stoves: use seasoned wood only (aged about a year). Burning freshly cut wood creates a chemical called creosote, which is bad for your lungs and builds up rapidly in the flue.

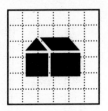

8

Fireplace

······················

Don't overlook the fireplace. Carefully check all the bricks and mortar joints on the facing. The weakest point is below the mantel and above the lintel.

Lintels and Mantels

The lintel is a heavy piece of metal that supports the bricks over the opening (Fig. 23). It's not surprising to find a mortar crack running in a zigzag pattern from the lintel to the mantel. Hairline cracks are common. But if there's a wide crack, say $1/8$ inch at the lintel, growing thinner as it rises, it could mean that the lintel is weak from rust and age and starting to sag. You know it won't get any stronger. Hold a straight edge up under the lintel to determine the severity of the sag. Lie on your back on the hearth and look up. Inspect the lintel. Replacing this is a major job.

Another thing to look for is whether any of the facing bricks are coming loose from the wall. Check to learn if the mantel is level. If it isn't, it could mean the whole fireplace unit has poor footing and is settling into the earth. If this is the case, the fireplace is independent of the floor, and you can

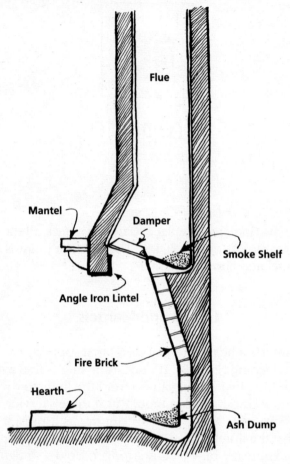

Figure 23
The Fireplace

notice the line of bricks at floor level and whether they maintain a straight and level line.

Sometimes the hearth is laid directly on the floor. If this is the case, notice if the floor is sagging, causing a crack where the hearth meets the vertical bricks. Then check below for the condition of the supports.

In many areas it's against the code to rest the hearth on the floor joists. If you find such a condition, don't worry, provided there is extra support directly beneath the hearth. The support may be posts, or it could be "doubled-up" joists.

Dampers

Use your flashlight to look inside, up the flue. Is there a damper? Does it operate? Try it. If there's no damper, it's a minus. It has been determined that in an average-size fireplace the heat loss without a damper, or with one wide open, is 14 percent. And not only that, but a slight draft of cold air persists in the wintertime, scuttling across the floor, drawn by the warm air escaping through the chimney. (This is the main cause of the common complaint of cold feet.) In the summer, insects enter the house through an open damper. In the old days, when fireplaces didn't have dampers, people used to put a piece of cardboard in the fireplace opening.

Bricks and Grout

With your screwdriver, jab at the firebricks. Note if they are loose. Test the grout between the bricks. In time it deteriorates. If enough grout falls out, the bricks will follow. After all, it's what holds them in. It's not catastrophic if you find loose bricks or missing grout. Nine times out of ten you can make the fireplace as good as new with an hour's work. Scrape out old grout with a screwdriver. Get a little vicious; this is not brain surgery. Clean it deep. From a building supply store buy some fireclay; the kind mixed with sand is best. Mix with water to a heavy paste or mud. With a broad knife or putty knife, force the mud into the cracks. If you're not good with the knife, use your fingers. But force the mud all the way in. Mud on top of mud. Let it dry for forty-eight hours before a fire is lighted. The slower and longer the curing period, the less chance of cracking.

Sometimes bricks are crumbly, cracked, chipped, loose, and falling out. These should be replaced. A mason should do this job. Get a price. All these figures will tell you what to offer for the house. At the same time, ask about installing a damper if the fireplace doesn't have one. The gravity kind can be installed in a ready-built fireplace.

Smoking

There's something good in everything, and the more you can see, the better for you. Those burned-out bricks and loose grout tell you that it's a good fireplace, for it has been much used, and who's going to use a smoky unit? Be suspicious of a clean, unused unit. Igniting a piece of paper to learn if it draws well isn't conclusive evidence that you're going to be able to sit around a fire and enjoy a long evening with brandy and backgammon. It may smoke enough to cure a ham.

It's difficult to determine whether a fireplace smokes each time it is used. Some of them are temperamental. But there are indications that will tell you if it is an inveterate smoker. Start by asking the owner. Honest people do exist. Look for carbon or black stains on the face above the lintel. Have stains been recently washed off? Has a metal shelf, canopy, or hoodlike affair been added? If so, it is there for one purpose only: the fireplace was a smoker and may still be. Often the hood cures the problem. But there are other ways to correct the fault if you don't like the looks of the hood. First make sure the chimney is not stopped up or practically choked by fallen bricks, a rather common situation. Note if surrounding trees or tall structures cause eddies down the flue. This frequently happens. The fireplace may predate a new building nearby, or the trees may have grown since the house (and fireplace) was built.

If none of these things are visible, you should next determine if the fireplace has the proper proportion between the size of the opening and the cubic area of the stack or flue. If you don't mind cluttering your head with figures, here is the rule of thumb for the proper proportion: the flue area is equal to $1/12$ the fireplace opening, if the flue is more than twenty-two feet high. If less than twenty-two feet, the flue area should be $1/10$ the opening. You can't do anything about the area of the flue once it's built, but you can increase the height to provide more draw. For a test, get a piece of sheet metal and wrap it around the top of the chimney, first removing the cap; hold it with wire, adding two or three feet to the height. If this cures the fault, erect something permanent. Another test is to cut down on the size of the opening. Build a fire and hold a piece of wood or metal across the opening at the top. Lower it until the fire stops smoking. Mark the lowest edge. This tells you how low the permanent opening should be if you choose to do this rather than adding to the chimney height. A mason could bridge the opening with bricks if you like. Or have a hood built and installed. Good luck. Enjoy the brandy.

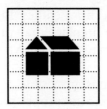

9

Plumbing and Sewage

....

If you keep your wits about you, you'll see strange things while walking around inspecting. In a two-story house, ask where upstairs bathrooms are located. Then look carefully at the ceilings beneath the bathrooms. You may see a stain or, worse, a spot where the paint is peeling. If this is the case, you can be almost certain of a bathroom leak. Don't let the sellers tell you it's the result of a champagne explosion and they left it there for sentimental reasons.

Bathroom Leaks

There are two common causes for bathroom leaks. One: the toilet seal has broken. Repairing this is not a major job. Two: careless showers. Water gets between the curtain and tub, runs down the side, and settles at the floor. When there's enough, it seeps through. If there's a glass sliding door on the tub, turn the shower on. Direct the stream against the door. Close the door and watch for water seeping out between tub rim and door seal. So you get a little wet. Sorry. If there are leaks, the door frame will have to be resealed. Another cause of leaks is the breaking of the seal between the faucets or tub spigot and the wall. There could be a hairline crack. You have to deflect water against the wall to detect this leak. Then get under the floor and look for water or water stains.

If there's a stall shower, a good test for a leak is to lay some paper over the drain and fill the shower pan with two or three inches of water. Let it stand for fifteen minutes or more, then go below to look for leaks. You're mainly testing the pan itself, where it meets the walls, and where the pan meets the drainpipe. In some states, this is a standard test used by termite inspectors. Afterward, let the water drain and check the drainpipes for leaks. Look carefully also around the shower opening. If the curtain has not done a good job, there could be leaks in that area.

One test for a broken toilet seal is to flush the toilet, then lean down and, using your flashlight, inspect the floor around the bowl. Try to move the toilet. Straddle it, grip the bowl with both hands, and try to tip it from side to side. It shouldn't move. If it tips slightly to one side, the seal could be broken. Check to see if the wood adjacent to the toilet is wet or swollen. You may not want to do it, but you can also rub your finger along the angle between the bowl and the floor to look for moisture. These tests are not conclusive, since the leak has to be severe for moisture to show up at floor level. But if the seal is broken, moisture will collect between the floor and the bowl. Dry rot will result.

If the moisture on the ceiling was not caused by toilet or shower leaks, it undoubtedly comes from a source pipe or drain, from either the tub or washbowl. This could be expensive to repair, for a portion of the floor will have to be removed. Think! If you still like the house, make an offer on condition that the leak is repaired. If it's your own house, repair it.

Of course, if you see the same sort of water stain, peeling

paint, or wood rot in a top-floor bathroom, the problem lies above you, in the roof. Some bathrooms are equipped with a vent that pierces the roof, and the metal flashing around that vent may have opened up. Go back to Chapter 4 for advice on inspecting roofs.

Water Pressure

While you're in the bathroom, turn on the tub water, leave it on, then turn on both faucets of the washbowl, keeping an eye on the tub flow. Note how much it diminished in force. Flush the toilet. Is there much loss of flow in the tub and washbowl when water starts filling the toilet tank? If the shower is separate, test that at the same time. Are you getting enough water for a shower, or just a trickle of irritation? If you've got two bathrooms in the house and more than one urgency, you can imagine what will happen in the morning when you're trying to shower. The same thing will happen to the shower when the kitchen faucet is turned on. If the flow is unsatisfactory, you can be certain the plumbing is galvanized steel.

Over the years, mineral deposits and rust have accumulated inside the pipes until there may be only a small opening left. This, of course, increasingly restricts the volume of water. The horizontal pipes collect mineral deposits more than the vertical pipes. Often, replacing the horizontal ones will provide all the water you need. If not, you can still replace the verticals.

But before you replumb, ask the water company to check the pressure at the main in front of the house and again at the point where the pipe enters the house. If there is a big difference in pressure, the pipe from the main to the house should be changed. Often these are very old pipes and a great deal of mineral deposit has built up inside them. It has happened

that a house has been replumbed with no appreciable increase in pressure, simply because the pipe from the main to
the house was poor.

Pipes and Joints

Sometimes miracles happen, but don't depend on them.
Those little valves you see beneath the washbowl, toilet, and
tub are called angle stop valves. They are natural traps (Fig.
24). Replacing them often helps the problem 50 percent.
Other culprits for collecting rust particles are elbows, mainly
the ones that turn from horizontal to vertical. Rust drops
down the vertical and rests in the ell, builds up, and constricts
the flow. These elbows are quite easily replaced. All these
measures aid the force of flow. Of course, the ultimate answer is to install copper pipes. Copper pipes are a superior
product and do not create rust buildup.

After you've run water, check the P traps for leaks. P traps
are the curved drains, usually chrome, beneath sinks and
lavatories (Fig. 24). Run your hand over them. Observe.
Check the angle stop valves for leaks. Remember to flush
every toilet in the house and turn on every faucet. This will
test not only for force of flow and volume but also for leaks in
the drainpipes and the toilet seal.

Faucets and Flows

Time how long it takes for hot water to arrive at the kitchen
faucet. If it takes much longer than ten seconds, it's probably
because the water heater is a long distance away. Perhaps
you can live with this delay, but you should know that it's a
waste of energy. The kitchen faucet is the most used item in
any home. A 1/2-inch pipe twenty-five feet long contains

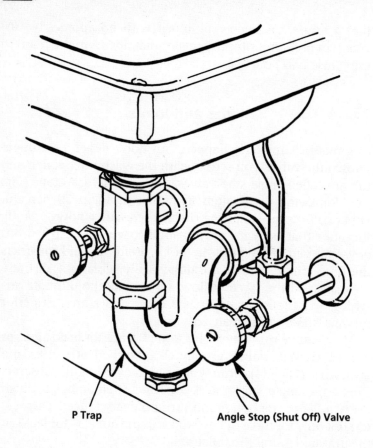

P Trap

Angle Stop (Shut Off) Valve

Figure 24
P Trap and Angle Stop Valves

more than two quarts of water. The water standing in that pipe has been heated once and allowed to cool. When you turn on the hot water faucet, that water is pushed out and wasted, then replaced by another half gallon that has been heated and left standing in the tank. This happens several times a day. Multiply that by the millions of homes with similar conditions, and you realize the vast amount of wasted energy and water. It would pay to move the tank closer to the center of the house or to insulate the pipes.

While turning on the faucets, did you notice that some of them leak from around the handle? Write it down. They should be repaired. Often this is the cause of moisture beneath the sinks or basins, for water gets between the faucet and the surface and drips. The cause of this is poor bonnet packing. Thousands of articles have been written on how to change washers to stop drippy faucets, but few mention bonnet packing. Changing washers won't prevent leaking bonnets. If you're going to do the job yourself, here is one simple remedy. Remove the old packing and wrap the stem with ordinary cotton string to fill the void of the bonnet. With this method there's no need to have a certain size of bonnet gasket. String can be wrapped to fit any size. It will last five years or more. You probably will never meet a plumber who doesn't carry a ball of cotton string. With that a plumber can meet most emergencies. He or she uses string many times in place of gaskets in the large chrome nuts on the drainpipes beneath sinks. You can too.

Sometime after testing all plumbing fixtures you're going to have to get beneath the house and crawl on your knees and walk on your elbows. In tight places you may have to lie on your back to look up at the underside of the bathroom. Curse if it helps. Take a screwdriver, flashlight, and patience with you. Look carefully for leaks beneath toilets, tubs, sinks, showers. If any wood is moist or stained, prod and poke with your screwdriver to detect if there is wood rot. If you find no leaks, you gain assurance. But if there are leaks, make a note that you want them repaired before you buy the house. If there is wood rot, check to learn whether a portion of the floor will have to be replaced.

How do you know where the toilet sets? Easy. Toilets have to be set directly above one of the large pipes you see disappearing through the floor. Almost always it is a four-inch pipe, usually cast-iron, but in old houses it may be lead, and in new houses, plastic. There may be two such pipes close together, but one of them is the vent pipe. If you can't determine which is which, look carefully for leaks around both of them.

Don't hesitate to buy a house in which the toilet seal is broken, giving you visions of unreasonable plumbing bills. A plumber can reset a toilet with a new seal in forty-five minutes. Or you can do it yourself in twice the time.

While under the floor, calculate the ease or difficulty with which you or a plumber could get to the pipes if trouble should occur and you need help (usually on Thanksgiving). This factor has a decided influence on the value of the house. Look for clean-out plugs in the drains. Clean-outs are plugs with square heads to receive a wrench, often at the ends of lines. Sometimes they are on a Y on verticals, or horizontals. If you see several of them, there's a built-in convenience (Fig. 25).

Water Heaters

Are the fresh-water pipes insulated? This is essential for houses in the Midwest, East, and North. Check the insulation. Add more if necessary. This is a case where too much does no harm, except to purse and back if you are doing it yourself.

There must be a water heater somewhere. Determining its age is difficult. Look for a tag with the date of installation. Can't find one? Not surprising, unless it's only two years old or so. Age and capacity are important, as well as quality. Glass-lined water heaters are the most common. You can expect ten to fifteen years' service from them. Monel- and copper-lined tanks will last longer. Tanks are always labeled so you will know which kind you have.

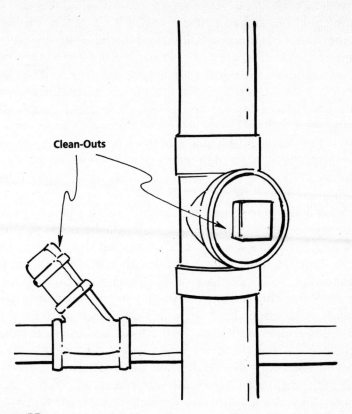

Clean-Outs

Figure 25
Clean-Outs

Start your examination by asking the owner if he or she knows the age of the heater. Time passes quickly, so add two or three years to the answer, unless you are shown the dated installation bill. Look carefully for moisture beneath. If there is some, be certain it isn't a drip from the drain valve, which is near the bottom. Put your hand on the end of the valve. No moisture? Then the tank is probably leaking. They don't cure themselves. The tank itself is inside the thin metal casing, plus an inch or so of insulation. There's no telling where the hole could be, and patching is out. If it's a gas- or oil-fired heater and the burners are pitted and corroded, it's an indication of age or of frequent heavy use. Its life expectancy has been shortened. Check the temperature setting. If it's at the hottest level, it could mean the tank has a difficult time providing water for the household. How many people are living there? What size is the tank? A thirty-gallon gas- or oil-fired tank should be adequate for three people, a forty-gallon for four. They have a high recovery rate, oil better than gas. Electrically heated tanks can't match them, so larger tanks are required.

Look at the pipe connections at the top of the tank. If heavy rust shows, it was caused by a leak. Maybe it has stopped leaking. Dig a little away, but be aware that you may start the leak again. It could be a rust-through spot, brought on by electrolysis. If copper pipes are attached to steel pipes an inch or so above the tank, there should be either an insulated union connecting the two or a short piece of brass pipe between copper and steel. In the trade the union is called "dielectric," and the point is to prevent electrolysis. There should also be a valve on the cold water side near the top of the tank so you can cut off the water in an emergency. And there should be a temperature relief valve on the hot water pipes or on the tank itself (Fig. 26). A pipe should lead from the valve to drain hot water to a safe place, preferably one that's exposed so you can spot telltale escaping water.

Gas- or Oil-Fired Water Heaters

A gas- or oil-fired tank will have a vent pipe. Check the pipe for firm connections and rust. There must also be combustion venting—fresh air leading to the area. If the tank is in an enclosed area there should be a three-by-six-inch hole cut into the door top and bottom, or a hole in the wall to the outside. Sometimes there's a hole in the floor to the crawl space, or air is brought in from the roof. Fresh air allows the

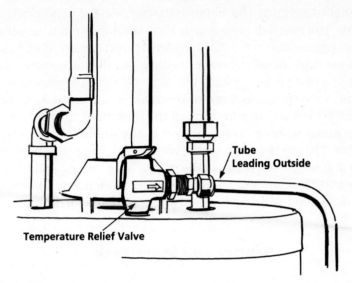

Figure 26
Temperature Relief Valve

flame to burn hotter with more efficiency. Check the gas or oil lines for leaks. Use a small paintbrush and apply detergent mixed with a little water to each fitting. Bubbles will appear with the slightest leak. Poor oil fittings will drip oil.

Electric Water Heaters

Electric water heaters don't have flues. They require 220 volts of electricity and must have their own circuit. Make sure there is water in the water heater before it's turned on. The size of the wire and circuit breaker depends upon the wattage. The average heater has two elements that heat alternately, usually 4,500 watts. Be sure the wire is the right size to accommodate the amperage of the breaker; check the installation instructions (see Chapter 6).

Gas- and oil-fired water heaters should be drained occasionally to get rid of the deposits that settle at the bottom of the tank. Too much deposit acts as insulation through which the heat has to pass to reach the water. The proper draining procedure is to cut off the water leading into the tank, then turn on one or two hot-water taps upstairs, attach a hose to the drain valve at the bottom of the tank, and open that valve. Allow the water to run through the hose until clear. If that's too much trouble, attach a hose to the drain and open the valve. That method stirs up the water more, but it's better than no draining at all. Incidentally, if you hear rattling and banging in your plumbing system, the cause is often deposits in the tank. A good draining is called for, or look into deliming.

Sewage and Septic Tanks

Most homes in the United States and Canada are served by municipal sewage systems that collect and treat household waste. To confirm that the house you're considering is one of them, just ask the seller for copies of sewer bills. If you want to be sure that the sewage pipes are intact, ask a municipal worker to check the drainage pipe to the street. A very healthy tree located along the path of the drainage pipe might be enjoying the nutrients provided by leaking sewage! Once waste reaches the municipal system, it's no longer your individual responsibility, though as a citizen you share the responsibility to have it treated properly.

Up to 50 million people live in homes not served by a municipal sewage system, however. Instead, their houses are equipped with domestic sanitary drain systems, involving septic tanks located on the property. This sort of system is more important for a prospective buyer to check because the costs of maintaining it will be your responsibility.

In domestic sewage systems, waste drains from the house through a distribution box into a septic tank. The waste stays in the septic tank long enough for powerful bacteria to break down the solids. Solids drop to the bottom of the tank and the remaining waste water is considered "partially treated." This fluid flows from the top of the tank into a leach field with pipes to distribute the treated water over a large area of ground. Bacteria in the soil will complete the task of purifying the treated water. This is a natural process. A properly maintained domestic sanitary drainage system can provide up to twenty years of service.

Ask the seller how old the house's domestic drainage system is; a system over fifteen years old may need replacing. Ask to see records of when the system was last pumped out. Find out the size of the septic tank. The minimum sizes are:

2 bedrooms: 750 gallons
3 bedrooms: 900 gallons
4 bedrooms: 1050 gallons

Adding rooms to the house may require enlarging the domestic drainage system or even "buying into" the municipal system instead. If you plan to expand, check with the local building and health departments on their requirements. While you're there, inquire about any documents that concern the system in the house you're considering.

Ask the seller to provide a map that shows the septic tank access opening and all other parts of the system. The septic tank should generally be 5 to 10 feet from the foundation of the house. As long as the leach field is located at least 100 feet away from any drinking water well, you shouldn't have to worry about contamination. Walk out to the tank and leach field. There should be no structures built over them. Check for sewer odors, excessive moisture, or foliage that appears to be extraordinarily healthy in spots. For example, a lawn with uneven growth that can't be explained by sun or other drainage may be evidence of a failed domestic drainage system.

Test the plumbing as you walk through the house. With somebody's help, flush all the toilets at once and watch how fast the bathtub drains, especially a tub on the first floor. Slow drainage is one sign of a blocked system. It doesn't take much to block some systems—even using a garbage disposal or the wrong kind of toilet tissue. Leach field lines plugged by toilet paper not designed for septic systems will have to be dug up and replaced. Unfortunately, a lot of domestic drainage systems have been accidentally destroyed like this. Make sure yours will give you years of service!

Finally, if you're seriously interested in making an offer for a house with a domestic sewage system, have a professional inspect the system. The buyer foots the cost of the bill, but a few hundred dollars is easier to pay than $20,000 for a new system.

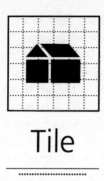

10

Tile

....

That nice tile job you saw in the bathroom looked new, shiny, entirely waterproof, and durable. But is it? If your family takes many showers, you want a high-quality tile job. The tile itself may be of good quality, but what method of application was used? That's the test. If it was a do-it-yourselfer's job to prepare the house for selling, beware; he or she undoubtedly used mastic and glued the tile to the wall. Even that could be all right, provided the wallboard is waterproof gypsum board or exterior plywood, or if a special waterproofing agent was applied to a nonwaterproof wallboard before the mastic was used.

Tile Application, or the "Mud Method"

The superior method of tile application is the use of mortar. Mud, it's called in the trade. The mud method is definitely not do-it-yourself. You should know the difference between mastic and mud so that you can determine what you're buying.

Using the mud method, a layer of asphalt felt is stapled to

the wall, then stucco wire, then floating screeds $1/2$ inch thick are attached. Next, mortar is applied and smoothed to the thickness of the screed boards. When this is properly cured, the tiles are applied, using a beating board to knock and press them into position, forcing them firmly into the mud on the walls. After suitable drying time, the grout is added to fill the cracks between the tiles. Sounds easy, doesn't it? It is, after about the fiftieth time.

Okay, so why is the mud method superior to the mastic? Because hairline cracks frequently occur in the grout between tiles, cracks so small you can't see them. Moisture gets in the cracks. If the tiles are glued on with mastic, the moisture could soften and swell the backing, thereby pushing the tiles off the wall. If hairline cracks occur in a mud job, the moisture has $1/2$ inch of concrete to get through before it reaches the wall, which has tar-paper protection. That's quality. No worries, unless you don't like the color of the tiles. Sorry; they're there to stay.

However, there are extra-thin tiles on the market, made primarily to be installed over existing tile walls. All that is required is that the existing tile be securely attached to the wall. Loose or nonceramic tile will not afford a proper base. These thin tiles come in two different forms, depending on the method of application. One has glue on the back with a protective paper. Simply strip off the paper and place the tile in position. The other is used with a special mastic that is applied to the wall before the tile is applied. In either case, grouting is done after all tiles are in position. So if you find purple, pink, or puce tile, you *can* do something about it.

Run the handle of your screwdriver over the tiles on a wall. As it bounces along, listen carefully for hollow sounds, which indicate loose tiles. A little tapping is good, also.

Mastic versus Mortar

How can you tell which method of application was used? You've probably figured it out already. With mastic, the tile is directly against the wall, and you can see this along the edge. The edge is curved (nosing tile), but the finished surface of the tile is 1/4 inch from the wall, maybe less. With mortar the tiles stand out more than 1/2 inch from the wall. Special round nosing tiles cover the borders, and these tiles touch the wall, but they're thick enough to cover the 1/2 inch of mortar.

If you find aluminum or plastic tiles, you've found trouble, generally. Many times these tiles are painted, so it's a little difficult to tell what they're made of. However, aluminum or plastic tile is thinner than ceramic tile. Look at the edge and you can tell the difference. If you're not sure, use the sharp point of your knife and test. Plastic and aluminum are soft. The reason they spell trouble is that no grout is used to seal between the tiles. Moisture can easily get between the cracks and soften the backing. Many people learned this too late, and that's why they painted them. They hoped to seal the cracks with the paint. Don't depend on it.

Countertops, especially in kitchens where standing water more easily seeps between tiles, are more vulnerable to damage if tiles are applied with mastic. Remember to jot down these points in your pro-and-con columns.

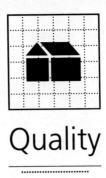

11

Quality

Home inspection is essentially looking for faults, but it is not all negative. While poking and prodding about, you may find hidden quality also. If you're buying, it's good to know where your money is going.

Hidden Quality

Like the difference in quality between a mud and mastic tile job, there are several other important differences worth mentioning between a carefully built house and a zip-zap piece of construction. Many people believe that the new and better fixtures and appliances are reserved for the rich and will not fit in an old house. That's wrong. Anything that's in an expensive house is available to anyone who is willing to spend a little more money, which buys economy in the long run. Quality adds up to more comfort and less trouble. Take faucets, for example. The best-quality faucet operates freely, consistently, and positively and seldom drips or spills water from around the handles. They're a pleasure to use. No cursing or frequent disassembling. There are toilets that flush silently and refill without a sound—entirely unlike the cataract of roaring water in a cheap one. There are furnaces that cannot be heard, yet the house is a uniform temperature all the time. Electronic filters or air cleaners can be added to any forced-air furnace. They draw and collect tiny dust particles that go right through ordinary filters into the furnace and are baked and blown right back into the house for you to breathe in and sneeze out. Another good product is a day-and-night thermostat, which automatically reduces heat during the night and increases it early in the morning. There are garbage disposals that emit a low hum no louder than the water running into the sink. There are doors that are heavy and close with a satisfactory finality, and light switches that are silent and don't interfere with the radio.

Bathtubs can make a big difference. A steel tub is thin and so is its porcelain surface; the porcelain cracks and flakes off more easily. Not so with a cast-iron tub. The latter will hold thicker porcelain for a much longer life. To tell the difference in tubs, rap the side with your knuckles. The steel tub is thin and rings, whereas the cast-iron is thick and makes no sound, like a rock.

The best toilet made will fit in a forty-year-old house, as will the best faucets. Furnaces can be made quieter by the use of insulating couplings or flexible fiber tubing on the cold air return or heat ducts. Solid doors will fit any opening. Locks fit any door. A good garbage disposal is heavily insulated and made with better gears and longer-lasting cutters. It does more work faster and is more durable.

The majority of the items mentioned above are the most-used items in any home. It pays to have them of good quality.

If you are remodeling extensively, think about these points. Give yourself a treat and live like the rich in your own old house. Remember, when you spend money for something you could have gotten more cheaply, it only hurts for a little while. After the pain is over, you'll be glad you suffered it.

Insulation

There is much talk about saving energy, and rightly so. We have to do better, and there's much we can do. All houses are someday going to need new appliances. When that time comes, if you live in an area where natural gas is the fuel please get pilotless appliances. When you consider the number of pilot lights that are burning in your home twenty-four hours a day, you get an idea of the amount of gas wasted each year in North America. This waste could all be stopped with pilotless appliances, and should have been a long time ago. In the meantime, matches still work.

Insulating a house properly will save more energy than any other program. But how much insulation is proper? Each climatic area makes different energy demands on a house. The building codes should be checked for recommendations. Asking an insulating company how much insulation you should have is like asking a Toyota dealer what make of car is good to buy. There are basic facts one should know about insulation. Once they are understood, you can make a wise choice and not be fooled by anyone.

R-Value

Insulation is measured in R-value, which simply means the ability to resist the passage of heat. All products have insulating value, some more than others. Anything dense, such as wood or concrete, is poor. Trapped air bubbles are good. The higher the R-value, the better the insulation. When buying insulation, learn the R-value per inch. Knowing that, you can determine how many inches of a product are required to attain the total R-value that is recommended in your area. Attics should have more than walls because heat rises. That's good for anyone inspecting a house because attics are easy to inspect and, if need be, easier to insulate than walls. More and more states now require insulation for new construction. If you're buying a new house, check the building code in your area for the required amount, then check the house to learn if the insulation is up to code. But remember that building codes are usually minimum requirements. It usually pays to have more than is required in the attic. Figure 27 shows one company's recommendations for R-value in the United States. These figures are not code requirements.

A typical wall is $3^5/8$ inches thick. That figure dictates the amount of insulation you can have in the wall. Different products, different value. Insulating the walls of an existing house is difficult because of the anatomy of a wall. Usually it is done by drilling a few hundred holes through the exterior siding and pumping in the product. If it is not done correctly and thoroughly, you've wasted your money. For instance, it's difficult to know whether all the spaces have been filled. When you consider that walls have diagonal bracing and fire stops (cats), you begin to understand that there can be many honeycomblike voids in a wall. It takes a plumb bob in the hands of a good worker to find and fill them all. Here again, reputable companies are important. One sure way of knowing that full insulation is added to a wall is to install new siding with an insulating backing. As a matter of fact, if the house you're buying has aluminum siding and you don't like the product, investigate closely before you tear it off. If it has Styrofoam backing, you'll be losing good insulation for your preference of wood over aluminum.

Ceilings and Roofs

The ceiling or roof is the most important area to insulate. You lose more heat per square foot through uninsulated ceilings than you do through walls. Overall you lose more through walls because there's more wall area. But as heat escapes through the ceiling, a draw effect is created. Cold air

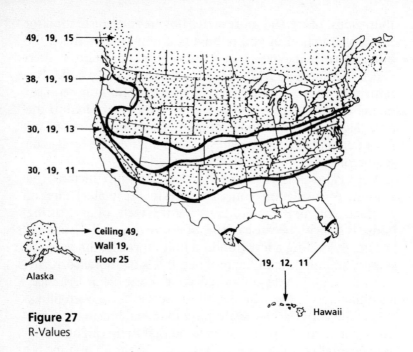

Figure 27
R-Values

entering through uninsulated walls, floors, and poorly weather-stripped doors and windows is drawn ceilingward. Stopping the escape stops the draft. This can be done in several ways:

1. Stop infiltration of cold air around doors and windows. (A poorly weather-stripped house has the equivalent of one square foot of open space in a wall. Brrr! $$.)
2. Insulate the ceiling heavily.
3. Insulate floors, ceiling, and walls.

Alternative 3 is the most effective. In most areas of the United States it is the only solution. But if the house you're buying or living in has poor insulation in the walls, you can help greatly by doubling up on ceiling insulation and doing something about the floors. The cost is much less than for insulating walls. And don't forget weather-stripping.

Houses that have no attic can be insulated. If rafters are exposed and the roof is good, you can consider adding insulation between the rafters and covering it with wood or gypsum board, leaving part of the rafters exposed. Or fill the entire area between the rafters and nail a new ceiling over the surface. If the roof is about gone (see Chapter 4), you can add insulation over the existing roof before applying the new waterproofing material. Thick shakes would have to be removed first. If it is a tar-and-gravel roof, rigid insulation is laid down on the existing roof, then plywood, then the new roof.

There are many new insulation products. Loose-fill insulation made of mineral fibers or cellulose flat pieces (manufactured from waste paper treated with fire retardants) is commonly used in the attic. Fiberglass is another common insulating material that works well and is safe when installed properly and not disturbed. It is often used in wall cavities and underfloor areas.

Urea-formaldehyde foam insulation (UFFI) is more troublesome. Though a good insulator, it can give off irritating formaldehyde fumes for years. UFFI has been banned in most areas, but many older houses still contain it. See Chapter 14 for more advice on dealing with a house that contains UFFI.

You hear and read much about insulating to save energy and money. It will do that, but the comfort achieved is just as valuable. In winter a well-insulated house does not have frequent and uncomfortable variables. The furnace rests longer between starts, and your body doesn't have to adjust so often. In summer, hot air is sealed out, and the air conditioning doesn't turn off and on so often.

Weather-stripping around doors and windows is important. Doors especially get rough treatment and get out of alignment. Flexible weather-stripping will take care of the voids that occur when two solid pieces come together. Caulking around door and window frames is necessary. The wood on the exterior warps, shrinks, swells, and works, leaving cracks. Use a caulking compound that doesn't harden, for it will move with the working lumber and keep a seal. So check carefully for weather-stripping and good caulking. Stop infiltration.

If a house in an area of freezing winters doesn't have double-pane windows, there must be good storm windows. Triple-pane is superior and should be considered if extensive remodeling is anticipated. It's becoming common practice to install double-pane windows in newly built houses. It should be the code. If the house you are buying has the built-in quality mentioned above, you can expect to pay for it, but you'll be happy you did.

Color is insulation also. Remember this: white reflects heat, black attracts and lets heat go right through. Aluminum foil is a good reflector. Houses painted white inside make energy-saving sense in cold climates. In hot climates, white roofs and walls save much energy by reflecting heat that would otherwise have to be thrown off by air conditioning.

Check for smoke detectors. If there aren't any and you buy the house, add a few. Ask the fire department for the best place to put them and follow the manufacturer's directions for installation, testing, and maintenance.

Solar Heat

If all the houses in the nation had solar collectors, the sun's energy would not be depleted by one BTU. It's that simple. The sun continually smiles at us and we ignore it.

Does the house you're inspecting have solar heat for water and/or space heating? A plus if it does. If not, consider it. Installing a solar hot-water system in your home can make you feel that you are doing something meaningful about conservation. Many people recycle bottles and papers, but with solar heat you *see* the results. That helps. It's a good feeling to find that after taking a shower or washing the dishes the gas water heater has not operated.

"How long will it be before it pays for itself?" is a common question. Who cares? One shouldn't always think about financial matters and whether the investment pays for itself. Think first about whether the investment is wise. Hauling bottles and papers to the recycling depot is time, trouble, and expense, but it's the thing to do. Solar heating is also an investment in the future. They'll both pay in the long run, in more ways than one. If you live long enough, and the sun shines brightly enough, a solar system will pay for itself, but in the meantime it's great to have plugged in the sun. Investing in the sun is a sure thing. It will always shine, but you have to be ready for it. Oil is expendable; sun is dependable.

Security

Security locks are important. Good ones are essential, or there is no security. Look at the door latch, which is the part that protrudes into the door jamb. If it has a small, half-round movable piece of metal on one side, you have a trigger bolt. That's better than a lock without one. The most secure lock is a dead bolt that requires a key from inside and out, both to lock and unlock. However, that type could be dangerous during a fire or other emergency if you can't find the key or children can't work the lock. Some building codes don't allow such locks because of this danger, so check with a local locksmith before buying. A mortise lock with buttons on the edge and a thumb turn on the inside is good, especially if the bolt is a long one. Short bolts are weak. Don't depend on a chain guard. Heavy snips can cut them with a snap.

Glass near a lock is not good. But if a dead-bolt lock is employed, the intruder could not reach in and unlock the door after breaking the glass. A key is required.

Glass sliding doors can be lifted out of the frame. A lock with a bolt set into a hole in the door frame is excellent. An alarm system is a bonus.

Windows are difficult. If you find steel bars covering windows and entrances, you've found either a house in a high-crime area or overprotective occupants. Bars are risky themselves because they prevent escape through the windows in an emergency. Look at neighboring houses. If doors and windows are heavily barred, it tells you something.

In any area a peephole on doors is helpful, as are exterior lights controlled from the bedroom. When in doubt, flick the switch. Better to be rude to indiscreet lovers than considerate to robbers.

12

Termites and Other Wood Destroyers

A buyer should conduct limited inspections for the obvious signs of termites, other damaging insects, and wood rot. This chapter describes the evidence left by several different pests. Unfortunately, many signs don't appear until the wood is already damaged. If you find weakened wood or its effects, such as a sloping floor over a hole-ridden pier, contractors should determine the amount of damage and estimate the costs to repair it. Clearly, termites and other creatures affect the value of a house.

Your most important tool for checking the strength of wood is a screwdriver. Poke hard at the suspect wood; it may look solid, but it could be hollow or full of holes. Strong wood will resist jabs. Beneath decks, houses, and carports you can really express yourself, but be gentle with finished lumber in decorative places, such as window sashes.

Termites

Sometimes termites can be as obvious as mud on a white wall. (In fact, the major sign of termites is small mud tubes built against the foundation.) Reading a few words about these little creatures' habits will be a big asset in understanding what to look for during an inspection.

Termites are tropical and prefer warm climates. In areas where winters are severe, termites are uncommon. Georgians will need to read this chapter carefully, but even some houses in the northern states and Canada are not entirely exempt. The increasing use of central heat has produced conditions quite comfortable for termites in some parts of the house; everyone should check carefully around the furnace.

A common name for termites is white ants, but that's a misnomer; although termites resemble ants, the two insects come from different orders of the insect kingdom. Some people say termites deserve their name because, if you leave them alone, they'll *terminate* your house.

Subterranean Termites

Termites that live in the soil are known as subterranean termites. They are common in the United States and are very destructive to houses. These termites do not expose themselves to the air, except in nuptial flights, but then they're only having fun, so who cares? They feed on wood, and if there isn't any food lying directly on the ground, they can build mud tubes up a foundation wall or pier to reach some. Subterranean termites travel back and forth in these tunnels, preparing a feast from pieces of lumber and moisture from the soil.

Therefore, look for mud tubes: dark brown lines about $1/4$ inch wide. Walk all around the exterior of the house, pulling away foliage and anything else that blocks your view. Even if only six inches of the concrete foundation is showing all around the house, that space allows you to spot termite tubes. You can examine the house exterior nearly as fast as you can walk around it. If you see any tubes, don't panic; the house isn't going to fall down on you, but you know you have a problem.

If the house's wood siding touches the ground, subterranean termites don't need to build tubes to feed. They can also enter a house through cracks in the foundation. Stucco houses, with a hard plaster exterior finish, pose a special problem if the stucco extends to the earth. Stucco doesn't stick very close to concrete, and termites often crawl up *between* the stucco and the foundation. If you are considering a house with such a stucco finish, you may want to call in a professional termite inspector before purchasing it.

In some eastern states metal termite shields may have been installed between the mud plate and the foundation (Fig. 28). Shields extend approximately two inches from the concrete at a 45-degree angle. They were used to prevent termites from secretly building mud tubes. The shields force the termites to build their tubes up and over the shield, which provides the owner with early evidence of their approach. You probably won't find shields on houses constructed after 1960. Check the condition of any shields you find. If they're rusted and deteriorated, or flattened against the wall, they're useless, and it would be better to depend on a termiticide applied by properly licensed professionals.

Now put on your old clothes to inspect under the house. A cap and gloves will help, for you should be as comfortable as possible in order to stay beneath the house and do a thorough job. Have a strong, dependable flashlight that won't go out on you when you get to the far end of the crawl space. Take a screwdriver and crawl in. Shine your flashlight along the edge of the foundation, piers, and pipes looking for termites' tubes. Look also for freestanding tubes coming right out of the soil.

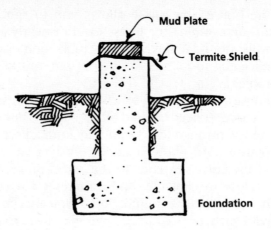

Figure 28
Using a Termite Shield

Wherever you see tubes, break them open and look for small gray-white insects. They won't hurt you. If there are no termites inside, they have probably evacuated; destroy the tubes because they can return. If you find termites, scrape away the tubes. The termites in the wood above will usually die because you have cut off their escape. However, the remaining termites in the soil may quickly rebuild their tunnels, so watch for new tubes.

Check all wood framing around any tubes with your screwdriver. Soft wood means the termites have destroyed the wood's strength. If you find a severe insect infestation, the homeowner should call pest control professionals. After all, they are the experts.

Termites usually swarm after the first days of spring. Seeing termites swarm out of the soil next to a house and fly away, you might think you're in luck because they're leaving. Not so: that house is definitely infested. Only the winged reproductive termites swarm to set up a new colony. The workers and soldiers remain, and keep eating. You may also find large numbers of termites caught in spider webs, or termite wings on windowsills. If so, it doesn't mean that house is infested yet, but you should look around for suspect areas of earth-to-wood contact, which would help them establish a home and survive.

Any actions to stop existing termite infestation should be taken by the owner. A home buyer should not accept a house with termites. Beware of houses being sold "as is": sellers who don't take responsibility for their houses either are lazy or have given up.

To prevent termites from consuming your house, make sure there's a six-inch clearance between any wood and the soil. Remove any roots, stumps, or wood debris near the house; they may be only scraps to you, but they're a feast to a termite. Clear foliage that touches the house; termites don't mind walking along a branch to reach their food. Periodically check the foundation for termite tubes.

While looking at the foundation or piers, you may see pieces of lumber left against the concrete, usually down low or in hard-to-reach places. This wood was probably used by the builder to form the concrete foundation and then proved difficult to remove. If you can't remove the wood, treat it with an insecticide or fungicide.

A concrete patio with wooden separators that touch the house siding is potential termite trouble. The boards should be cut off two inches from the house and the space filled with concrete. If the patio runs along the foundation of the house, it is a good idea to chemically treat two inches of soil between the patio and the foundation edge.

If your house does become infested with termites, the safest course is to hire a pest control company. You can also buy a recommended termiticide and treat the infested soil yourself. Most of these chemicals are not good to breathe, so wear a respirator and protective goggles while applying them. Pour the termiticide into the soil next to the foundation from a small spout, and it will prevent termites from building more tubes through the treated soil.

Remember that termites and other wood-consuming insects make no distinction between a handmade house of distinction and a prefab tract home. Only the care that owners put into their homes can stop them. Subterranean termites get the most blame for damaging houses, and they deserve it. But there are other culprits, too.

Dry-wood Termites

The dry-wood termite is a slow-acting but determined creature that is common in the southern coastal areas. It needs no soil contact. This termite likes redwood and oak but won't turn up its nose at any other wood. It riddles wood with holes and shoves out easily recognizable, sandlike pellets. Look for these pellets along baseboards or outside at the base of a wall, beneath floors, and especially in attics— damage generally occurs in the upper portions of a house.

Once a dry-wood termite invasion has occurred, it's best to contact a pest control operator. A general infestation requires tenting the entire house with plastic and inserting a poison gas: fumigation. Because this treatment leaves no residual protection, another infestation can occur.

If the insects have burrowed into only one or two boards, however, you can successfully treat the area with a liquid insecticide. Contact your local hardware store for an approved product, and once again, follow the manufacturer's instructions. Although chlordane and heptachlor were once recommended, they are no longer available and should not be used by anyone!

Damp-wood Termites

The damp-wood species of termite is found mostly in the northwestern states. Larger than the subterranean or dry-wood type, the damp-wood termite lives primarily in decay-

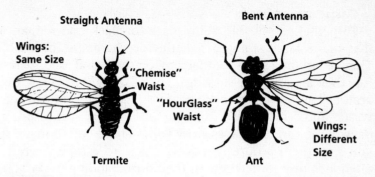

Figure 29
Common Wood Destroyers

ing wood but may move on to sound wood, provided it finds sufficient moisture. These termites are often found in decks, beneath bathrooms where leaky plumbing has caused the wood to decay, along eave lines, and in lumber stored in wet soil beneath a house. The ends of roof rafters are especially vulnerable. To control damp-wood termites, first get rid of the moisture, then the old wood. Finally, treat the remaining wood with a recommended termiticide.

Other Wood-Destroying Insects

Ants or termites? They both have winged forms, and you'll see both coming out of the soil or on windowsills. But the ant has an "hourglass" waist, whereas the termite has a bulky "chemise" waist (Fig. 29). The wings are also very different: the termite has four wings the same size; the ant's hind wings are smaller than its front ones. One more point: the ant's antennae are bent, but the termite's are straight.

Carpenter Ants

Carpenter ants are big, shiny black (or black-and-red) ants that make large, smooth galleries or chambers in wood. They're building nests, not feeding on the wood, and therefore they discard little shavings. Look for sawdustlike debris around baseboards and other areas. Ants feed on kitchen wastes and can be seen searching for food. On warm spring days, some carpenter ants grow wings and fly off to mate; if you spot them around windows trying to escape, there is often a colony somewhere in the house. Finding the nest is the problem. If you can locate it, try a carpenter ant insecticide from the local hardware store. If that doesn't work, call the professionals.

Powder-Post Beetles

Another creature in the entomological world that does tremendous damage to a house but leaves conspicuous traces is the powder-post beetle. A good name, for it turns wood into powder. These beetles riddle the surface of wood with round holes that can make your entire basement or attic look as if it has been used as the backboard for a beginners' dart game. The holes you see are made when larvae reach the adult stage and bore out of the wood. By the time the holes appear, you've had several years of pupal development going on within your house.

When a subfloor becomes riddled with tiny holes, the floor feels weak and springy. Strike the wood with your hand, and you'll see dust fall out of the holes. Once in a while you'll find the powder accumulated in little piles beneath infested lumber. Powder-post beetles get into furniture, too, literally reducing an antique to a shell of its former self. Look for these pests in attics and basements mostly, although they can appear anywhere.

If the infestation is general, the best remedy is to contact a pest control operator. Minor problems can be treated with an insecticide from your local hardware store. Just as important as discovering any pest is determining how much damage it has done. That's what this inspection is all about. So once again, jab and pry at the infested lumber to ascertain how extensively it has been weakened.

Old-House Borers

As its name implies, the old-house borer is another wood-destroying insect. While the larvae are boring away, they make a rasping or ticking sound. You can hear them, but visual evidence comes only after much damage is done. The adult departs, leaving behind a 1/4-inch broad oval hole in the wood.

Carpenter Bees

Carpenter bees are large black-and-yellow insects that look like bumblebees but have different habits. Carpenter bees bore into wood to make a home for their young. Look at porches, garages, sheds, railings, decks, roof overhangs, outdoor furniture, and wood fences. The holes are 1/2 inch across, with galleries inside the wood that make attractive nesting sites for the following year. An occasional hole won't weaken the wood, but enough of them will. The female, not the male, will sting. Most common insect aerosols are effective for control. Spray it in the holes and plug them with putty. Do so after dark to reduce your chance of being stung.

Wood Rot

While looking for termites and other insects, keep an eye out for wood rot (also called dry rot—see page 20). It is very common and is found everywhere there's a combination of wood, moisture, and poor ventilation. Basements or crawl spaces are especially vulnerable. Furthermore, although such places may be dry during your inspection, when moisture gathers the fungus will start to grow again.

Look for wood rot under eaves, around windows, and beneath plumbing fixtures. Inspect decks, especially where wood meets concrete. Poke the wood with your screwdriver. Remember: *Moisture on wood where no air circulates produces wood rot.* Whenever you see dark spots on wood, be suspicious. Sometimes white fungus grows on wood, and often the wood swells. In either case, the wood is probably soft for several inches.

If you find wood rot, prevent further moisture from reaching the area and apply a recommended fungicide from your hardware store. But if the damage is severe enough to have weakened wood that supports either part of the house or you (i.e., in a floor or a deck), that piece of wood will have to be replaced. Unfortunately, this usually occurs in hard-to-reach places, making the job slower and more costly. Damaged wood should be replaced with wood that has been commercially treated, available at most lumberyards.

Sometimes you'll find wood rot on less important areas, such as window sashes, deck railings, and door and window trim. Often there will be only a small amount beneath bathrooms, sinks, porches, and steps, or around the bathroom baseboard. To remedy such situations, there are good products on the market. One is an epoxy that, when inserted into the rotted wood, will be absorbed, fill all deteriorated fibers, and cling fast to good wood. It dries hard and permanent. It can be drilled, sanded, and painted. Some termite inspectors like to think no such product exists, but boat owners know more about wood rot than anyone, and they use it. Ship chandleries carry the product, as do hardware stores. Ask for Rot-Cure, Git-Rot, Calignum, or something similar. Take advantage of science, but don't forget common sense. To prevent wood rot, make sure that you have plenty of underfloor and attic ventilation, and that there is no standing water under the house.

In conclusion, respect termites and other wood destroyers, but don't fear them. Sure, they do damage, but houses rarely fall down because of termite infestation. Follow the six rules below and relax.

1. Use your head, your eyes, and your screwdriver.
2. Keep moisture out of places where it shouldn't be.
3. Keep wood away from soil.
4. Make sure the underfloor and attic areas are properly ventilated.
5. Make periodic inspections.
6. Apply chemicals to the soil around the foundation, following the manufacturer's instructions, but remember: Large jobs should be left to the professionals.

Good luck.

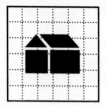

13

How to Interpret a Termite Report

Figure 30 is a replica of a California termite report. (Infestation by all three kinds of termite is common there.) They're not much different in other states. Listed in the squares at the top are the various faults that could be found on the property, but only those marked with an X indicate which ones were discovered. Let's go through them and see what was found, and define the terms.

Subterranean termites were found, but no dry-wood termites. Next, fungus, or dry rot, was found, but fortunately, no powder-post beetles. Then comes faulty grade level, which is checked. The term should be "faulty earth level," which means that the distance between earth and wood is not great enough. Most states require two inches of foundation above the earth on the exterior. Next is earth-to-wood contact, and this, as you know, is prohibited. No damp-wood termites were found. The shower leaked; this would be a stall

STANDARD STRUCTURAL PEST CONTROL INSPECTION REPORT
(WOOD-DESTROYING PESTS OR ORGANISMS)
This is an inspection report only - not a Notice of Completion.

ADDRESS OF PROPERTY INSPECTED	BLDG. NO. 27	STREET LOMITA	CITY Mill Valley, CA CO. CODE	DATE OF INSPECTION 9/26/77

FIRM NAME AND ADDRESS	
MORPHEUS TERMITE CONTROL ALTO, CALIFORNIA	Affix stamp here on Board copy only ↓ A LICENSED PEST CONTROL ↓ OPERATOR IS AN EXPERT IN HIS FIELD. ANY QUESTIONS RELATIVE TO THIS REPORT SHOULD BE REFERRED TO HIM.

FIRM LICENSE NO. 13	CO. REPORT NO. (if any) 726	STAMP NO. 1226

Inspection Ordered by (Name and Address) Mary Twichell
Report Sent to (Name and Address) 27 LOMITA, Mill Valley, CA.
Owner's Name and Address Pat Heyman
Name and Address of a Party in Interest Marlys Cheyne, 500 Wall Street, Seattle, Washington
INSPECTED BY: Mark Hoffman   LICENSE NO. 717   Original Report ☑   Supplemental Report ☐   Number of Pages

YES	CODE	SEE DIAGRAM BELOW	YES	CODE	SEE DIAGRAM BELOW	YES	CODE	SEE DIAGRAM BELOW	YES	CODE	SEE DIAGRAM BELOW
X	S	Subterranean Termites		B	Beetles-Other Wood Pests		Z	Dampwood Termites		EM	Excessive Moisture Condition
	K	Dry-Wood Termites	X	FG	Faulty Grade Levels	X	SL	Shower Leaks		IA	Inaccessible Areas
X	F	Fungus or Dry Rot	X	EC	Earth-wood Contacts		CD	Cellulose Debris	X	FI	Further Inspection Recom.

1. SUBSTRUCTURE AREA (soil conditions, accessibility, etc.)	See below #1
2. Was Stall Shower water tested? Yes Did floor coverings indicate leaks? Yes	
3. FOUNDATIONS (Type, Relation to Grade, etc.) Concrete-F.G. #4	
4. PORCHES . . . STEPS . . . PATIOS #3 and #4	
5. VENTILATION (Amount, Relation to Grade, etc.) Adequate	
6. ABUTMENTS . . . Stucco walls, columns, arches, etc. None	
7. ATTIC SPACES (accessibility, insulation, etc.) Not inspected	
8. GARAGES (Type, accessibility, etc.) None	
9. OTHER	

DIAGRAM AND EXPLANATION OF FINDINGS (This report is limited to structure or structures shown on diagram.)

General Description_____ Two and one half story rustic A-frame residence.

(1.) SUBSTRUCTURE: Sub-area, partially improved. Wooden platform is inaccessible on underside. Earth wood contact where dirt bank has fallen against the back wall. Evidence of termite infestation noted.

RECOMMENDATION: Remove wooden platform and saturate earth with a soil toxicant. Replace platform on masonry supports . Remove earth from back wall. Treat wood with approved chemical. Replace all infested wood with new wood.

(2.) SHOWER: Stall shower pan was tested according to prescribed method and was found to leak.

RECOMMENDATION: Remove shower pan and adjacent two rows of tiles. Install new shower pan. Replace bottom two rows of tile. Color match as close to existing tile as possible.

(2A) LOWER SHOWER: Lower shower is on concrete slab. No water test to pan was made as under area inaccessible. Rug near shower shows evidence of moisture. This due to improper sealing of shower door.

RECOMMENDATION: Replace shower door with new. Safety glass required. No replacement of rug allowed for in this report.

(3.) DECK: The posts supporting the deck exhibit fungus damage at the base. Some posts are imbedded in the soil.

RECOMMENDATION: Cut off the posts to good wood. Install masonry bases.

(4.) STEPS: Faulty grade level exists at base of front steps.

RECOMMENDATION: Remove earth to prescribed distance.

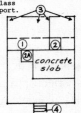

Figure 30
A Termite Report

shower, separate from the tub. No cellulose debris (an imposing phrase for loose scraps of wood that termites might feed on) was found. Nor was there excessive moisture, so drainage was good. However, there were inaccessible areas. This is important and explains the last square: further inspection is necessary. Termite inspectors aren't required to remove boards and gain access to otherwise inaccessible areas. If they can't get into a certain place and they feel it should be inspected, they recommend further inspection at additional cost.

Next on the report are nine categories that are self-explanatory. After that is a diagram of the house and garage, together with text explaining in detail where the faults were found and the recommendations to correct them. The numbers in the text refer to the numbers in the sketch. A cost sheet was also included.

Termite Clearance

You've probably heard the term "termite clearance" and wondered what it meant. It means that a licensed termite inspector guarantees that the house is free of all infestations and meets the state specifications. Only a licensed inspector can give a clearance. In the case above, the cost to do the work was $1,400. A clearance is issued by a company if the work is done according to their report. You don't have to hire the inspector to do the work before a clearance is issued. After you have a report, you have a guide; you can do the work yourself or hire a carpenter to do it. But it will take another inspection before the clearance can be issued. In some states it's not called a clearance but rather a certificate, which states that termites are absent or that treatment has been completed.

A growing number of loan agencies require a home buyer

to have a clearance before any money is loaned on the property. In such a case, the loan company withholds the amount the termite company says it will cost to clear the property. Let's say it's $1,400. The loan company puts that amount in escrow. You move into the house and you have the termite report. It tells exactly what has to be done to clear the property. If you can do the work yourself, so much the better. If you want to gamble, hire another company for another opinion. You may save yourself some money. There's frequently a big difference in opinions. Some inspectors are more lenient than others, some more careless, and some can see a much easier way of correcting faults, making the job less costly. Or ask your agent to recommend good contractors or carpenters who could do the work. Any agent who is worth his or her salt has a list of licensed pest control workers who are capable and who understand termite work. After the work is done, you hire a licensed inspector to check the work and grant a clearance. Then the escrow company will release the $1,400. In many cases the company will release the money on a guarantee from a contractor.

In all cases, talk with the original inspector before doing anything. Explain your circumstances. Frequently they'll show you what portion of the work you can do yourself, leaving the more difficult and sophisticated jobs for them. Removing earth is work; it won't hurt you to do it. If you do level with the inspector and he isn't helpful, get another one. You shouldn't deal with uncooperative people anyway. Don't worry that he will alert other inspectors to refuse you a clearance. There's so much competition in this business that you can easily get another inspector to examine your job and issue a clearance. Remember to watch out for "sweetheart" arrangements.

Let's take a case where you don't need a clearance. In your agreement the seller will pay $1,000 toward termite work. The report shows faulty grade level, some dry rot, termites in one corner, and excessive moisture in the crawl space beneath the floor. You now know how to take care of those things, and you're not lazy. Tell your agent you want the $1,000. The agreement doesn't stipulate the money has to go to a termite company. Put it in the bank and let it draw interest while you're working around the house.

In nearly all cases the buyer pays for the inspection report. You may be buying a house "as is." The seller will not pay anything toward repair work. He can do that. Most states do not require a termite inspection. But that doesn't stop you from getting one. After it arrives, study it closely and check it against the house to learn if the assertions made are accurate. If you have doubts, call the inspector. Make him prove them. Keep in mind that as a rule termite inspectors are looking for work. They are contractors who make a living doing repairs, not doing inspections. Some are fair and honest; you should be able to find one.

Needless to say, if the house is infested with dry-wood termites or powder-post beetles and has to be tented and fumigated, that's not a do-it-yourself project. But get several bids for the job.

Now a word in defense of termite inspectors.

The criticism most frequently heard is that they are too strict, especially on old houses that were built before so much was known about infestations and how to avoid them. Many recent building codes require termite prevention, so houses built before the new laws were written contain many violations of the present codes. Can old houses be exempt, as they are for, say, electric wiring? No. This is one case where the laws are retroactive. So don't blame the inspector. He has to report all violations of the present state pest control board specifications on old houses as well as new. But it's a two-way street. If you're buying, you want a strict report; if you're selling, you may complain.

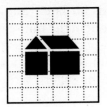

14

Environmental Hazards

The thought of environmental hazards in a house—asbestos, lead, formaldehyde, radon, toxic chemicals—can produce a lot of anxiety, in both you and the seller. You, of course, deserve a safe home and full knowledge of any potential dangers. The seller may fear that an environmental hazard will prevent the house from being sold and perhaps require costly cleanup. While you are walking through a house, express your concerns to the owner. A seller who tries to patronize you or changes the subject is a seller to be wary of. Some homeowners, however, may not realize their houses could be dangerous. All of the hazardous materials discussed here were considered normal, even beneficial, for homes before their dangers were recognized. So ask questions, and verify the answers.

Fortunately, according to the Environmental Protection Agency (EPA), most homes are free of environmental hazards, except old lead paint. To maintain this level of safety, some real estate contracts require the seller to certify that the house is free of some hazards.

This chapter introduces techniques for spotting potential

environmental hazards for later testing. Some of these tests require taking pieces out of the house or even more elaborate procedures. Before inspecting a house for potential environmental hazards or taking samples for further analysis, you should always obtain the seller's written permission.

Asbestos

Asbestos is a fibrous mineral found in rocks and soil throughout the world. It has some valuable properties, such as stifling fire and insulating, and has been used in hundreds of products through the centuries. Doctors now recognize that inhaling microscopic asbestos fibers can increase a person's risk of lung cancer (especially in smokers) and other deadly diseases. The dangers of asbestos were not known for a long time because these illnesses can take years to develop.

Asbestos fibers have almost been eliminated from new products. In older homes, however, there are still a few places that may contain asbestos fibers and should be of concern to the home buyer.

If you find material that you suspect contains asbestos, the first step is to have it tested. Look up "Testing Laboratories" in the local Yellow Pages. You will be given details over the phone on how to remove samples safely (if you can) and transport them to the lab. With solid construction material, you would normally remove a penny-sized sample, trying not to ruin the appearance of the house, and seal it in a sandwich bag. If you don't feel comfortable taking the samples yourself, ask the laboratory for names of people who will do it for you. You can expect to pay up to $50 per sample for testing.

Neither you nor the seller should ever rush to remove asbestos material. Asbestos within solid material poses very little danger unless it is disturbed. Only when asbestos fibers are already loose must they be removed quickly, by trained professionals.

Sprayed Ceiling Finish

If the ceiling finish looks like cottage cheese, you could be standing under asbestos-containing material. Asbestos fibers were used in spray finish until 1982. All ceilings sprayed prior to this date should be checked by a professional tester.

Do not try to take a sample from a sprayed ceiling! Scraping the asbestos-laden material off with a spatula could fill the air with asbestos fibers. They are so light that a fiber dropped from eight feet will take three days to hit the floor. You could end up with millions of microscopic fibers in your carpet, curtains, ventilation system, and, ultimately, in your lungs! Instead, contact a testing laboratory.

If the sprayed ceiling finish turns out to contain asbestos, you and the seller should seek estimates for the professional removal and disposal of the material. Although you may choose to leave the ceiling alone at this time, future remodeling may be more difficult. In 1992 proper removal and disposal costs of sprayed ceiling finish material ranged from $6 to $18 per square foot.

Furnace Duct Wraps

Visit the furnace room. Ducts, heat runs, or the large pipes that distribute conditioned air throughout the house must be inspected. Check ducts on the outside of the house as well. Pipes wrapped with a white material that looks like plaster of paris, with a solid gray material inside a canvas finish or with corrugated material, may contain asbestos fibers.

Furnace duct wrap can be left alone if the material is not torn. Any kind of rip in the material is potentially dangerous, however. Ask a heating and air conditioning contractor to recommend a qualified person to make the appropriate repairs.

Exterior Siding and Roofing

Siding that has a "manufactured look" may contain asbestos. Wood, masonry, metal, and plastic sidings are generally asbestos-free. Exterior siding that contains asbestos is not a health threat because the fibers are safely tucked inside the layers. However, future expansion plans might be hampered by having to cut into, remove, and dispose of the asbestos-laden siding. Contact a local siding or roofing contractor for an appraisal of your particular situation.

Insulation

Insulation is hard to check during a casual inspection. Although many insulation products contain no asbestos fibers, a prudent home buyer should ask the seller for permission to remove a sample of insulation material for testing at a lab. If the insulation contains asbestos, you should consult a professional who can check the air quality in the house.

Vinyl Flooring

If you want a vinyl floor to be tested, take a sample that includes the mastic used to secure it. A vinyl floor in good condition is best left alone. Proper removal and disposal of asbestos-laden flooring and the mastic may be prohibitively expensive. Sanding the floor will release asbestos fibers. Instead, new flooring should be installed over the asbestos-laden floor. However, you would have to disclose the fact that your home contains asbestos to the next potential buyer.

Lead

Records dating back to the fourth century B.C. document the health problems associated with exposure to lead. Absorbing too much lead can cause brain damage, especially in infants and young children. Lead pipe was used in Rome's water distribution system. Some historians have even wondered if the fall of the Roman Empire was caused by lead in the people's drinking water!

According to the EPA, two-thirds of the houses constructed before 1940 contain lead-based paint, as do one-third of the houses built between 1940 and 1960. How can you ascertain whether the house you are interested in buying is lead-free? Let's begin with the type of pipe used to convey the water throughout the house.

Plumbing

Look for galvanized pipe in the underfloor area of the house, the attic, or the attached garage. Galvanized pipe is the color of a nickel. If you find either galvanized or plastic pipes, you can assume the drinking water is free from harmful amounts of lead. However, if you find pipe that has the same color as a tarnished copper penny, you may very well have "leaded" water. Plumbers installing copper pipe and fittings must solder the pieces together, and until a few years back their solder contained a high concentration of lead. Ask to have both cold and hot water samples tested.

If test results show that the house's water contains lead, one option is to replace the entire plumbing system. Replacement costs vary according to the difficulty of reaching all of the pipe, including the line from the house to the water supply. Asking several plumbing contractors to submit bids for pipe replacement will give you a good idea of what to expect.

Some authorities advise people to simply let the tap water run for fifteen seconds before using it, sending the water that has been soaking in the lead-contaminated pipes down the drain. This method of avoiding leaded water will obviously increase your water bill and wastes water. Instead you may install a water treatment system to remove lead.

Lead Paint

Paint containing lead was taken off the market when studies determined that it is dangerous for humans to inhale the paint dust (created by sanding) or swallow paint chips (lead is temptingly sweet). According to the U.S. Department of Housing and Urban Development, removal or encapsulation is warranted if paint contains 0.5 percent lead by dry weight or 1 milligram per square centimeter by X-ray fluorescence.

In some states it is illegal for children under a certain age to live in a house with lead paint. If you have children, have the painted areas inside the house checked. One method of testing is to apply a solution of sodium sulfide to the paint. You can purchase sodium sulfide from a chemical distributor, found in the Yellow Pages. If the surface turns black, you know there is lead in the paint. Sample an unobtrusive area—not the center of the front door! Ask the seller's permission first, of course.

If you find lead paint inside the house, there may be other regulations governing its sale: if you sell the house later, you will have to disclose to potential buyers that it contains lead paint. Lead paint may not necessarily pose a threat, however. Problem areas could be wallpapered or otherwise protected. A door or a window frame coated with lead paint can be removed; in fact, opening and closing such a window can cause the paint to be ground into hazardous leaded dust. Bear in mind, however, that future remodeling will require extra care and expense, up to $20,000. Major renovations will include the costs of removing and disposing of materials coated with lead paint. All removal work should be performed by properly trained contractors, and the house will be no place for anyone to live until the project is complete.

A recent exterior paint job, with no flaking, is a real plus for you. Leave the paint alone and you won't have a problem. Older lead paint on the outside of a house tends to become chalklike. Lead paint dust ends up on the ground, and toys left in the "leaded" dirt could spell trouble for small children. Planting pyracantha or other hardy shrubs around the foundation will keep kids and some pets away from paint dust and chips.

Lead in Soot

Another source of lead contamination comes from auto and truck exhausts. A house located under a freeway will be coated with sooty fallout from vehicles passing by. The home buyer can look forward to the repetitive task of wiping the toxic soot off any surfaces exposed to the outside air. Soot can also end up inside the furnace, causing repeated exposure to lead.

Formaldehyde

Formaldehyde is a colorless, odorless gas that can cause skin rashes, breathing problems, watery eyes, or burning sensations in the eyes, nose, and throat. Animals have developed cancers when exposed to formaldehyde, but studies have not proved that formaldehyde exposure causes cancer in people.

Several types of construction materials can emit formaldehyde, including some plywood and permanent-press draperies. However, any gas from these sources dissipates after about five years. Unless a house contains new curtains, cabinets, or furniture, concerned buyers may simply rely on a consumer testing kit obtained from the local public health department or local chapter of the American Lung Association. Testing options for formaldehyde in the air range from consumer kits (costing $40 and up) to hiring an industrial hygienist.

More worrisome is urea-formaldehyde foam insulation

(UFFI), which was once widely used. It contains large amounts of the gas. Search the house walls for thick, white foam insulation. Begin by turning off the electricity and removing a few electric receptacles or light switch plates. Look deep inside the walls. Poke around using a bamboo chopstick. If the walls contain fiberglass insulation or no insulation, you can rest assured the home is free of formaldehyde-laced foam. If you pierce something that feels and sounds like Styrofoam, however, further testing is warranted. Be wary of a house containing UFFI: it can torment occupants for years, and the insulation can't be removed without ripping down the walls.

Some homeowners faced with the presence of UFFI in their houses have installed sophisticated ventilation systems to prevent the gas from accumulating in dangerous amounts. If you see such a system, ask the seller for records showing when it was installed and its capacity. Such a ventilation system should not rule out buying the house unless you're particularly sensitive to formaldehyde, but the owners should be candid about why it was installed.

Radon Gas

Tens of thousands of homes have been reported to contain radon gas, a natural radioactive gas that seeps up from underground deposits of uranium. Radon cannot be detected by one's senses. It can enter homes through the walls and floors of foundations, floor drains, and other voids created by pipes or ducts in the underfloor area of the house. Drinking water obtained from wells can also contain radon gas.

Prolonged exposure to radon gas can cause lung damage without the victim knowing it. It is suspected of causing up to 30,000 cancer deaths each year and may be the leading cause of lung cancer among nonsmokers. The question of what is considered an acceptable level of exposure has not been answered at this time.

You may wish to retain an expert to test a house for radon gas levels. According to a recent survey, the cost of analyzing a test sample ranges from $75 to $150. Houses located adjacent to each other may have different test results. If radon gas is detected, there are ways to reduce the seepage into the home and prevent it from building up inside. A ventilation system placed under the house to vent out the gas is one of several different solutions offered by professionals.

Safe Drinking Water

If the house takes water from a reservoir or other large system (serving more than twenty-five houses), the water is probably safe. Indeed, American metropolitan drinking water is the safest in the world. Your primary concern should be the pipes in the house and from the street to the house.

Small systems and wells are more vulnerable. Approximately 50 percent of Americans depend on groundwater as their source for drinking water. Pollutants, pesticides, and fertilizers can enter the system. Underground gasoline or home heating oil tanks can leak. Groundwater is also susceptible to leaking septic tanks, cesspools, and leach lines in domestic sewage systems.

If the property you're looking at depends on a well, have the water tested. Take both hot and cold water samples after the water has run through the tap for a few minutes. Contact a local laboratory for sample collection, instructions, and testing fees. You can expect fees ranging from $50 to $250, depending upon how extensive the testing is. There are over eighty contaminants regulated by the EPA. If you choose a house with any sort of underground water supply, plan to test the drinking water every year.

To minimize the chances of water contamination, study any tanks on the property. Have them checked to verify that they aren't leaking. A new home buyer automatically becomes responsible for underground tanks. Groundwater very close to an industrial site could be tainted with its waste. The local office of the EPA should be able to identify hazardous waste disposal sites for you.

Stored Chemicals

Homeowners accumulate a wide variety of chemicals over time—paints, household cleaners, motor oil, antifreeze—and many of these are toxic. The most innocently stored material can become a threat if it enters your soil or water supply. In any event, you shouldn't have to deal with these leftovers!

Make sure the seller will dispose of any chemicals before moving out. Check the corners of the garage and basement with the seller to ensure that no containers will be forgotten. If you find containers with missing labels, the seller should take responsibility for identifying and disposing of the substances properly. Disposal should follow the directions on the containers; some labels may even include a toll-free number to call for advice. Pouring these substances down the drain could result in a nightmare.

If you see large puddles of oil and grease on the concrete slab of the garage, the soil beneath may already be contaminated.

Finding Help

You should expect a home free of toxic chemicals and other dangers. Be sure to address environmental hazards when you make a deal with the seller. Ask the seller for copies of the results of any tests that have been performed. Later, after you have had the house tested and any hazards removed, you can advertise it as being "environmentally safe."

The cost of tests is generally absorbed by the buyer; however, it won't hurt to ask the seller to share the cost. Laboratory analysis fees might be more palatable if you consider them an investment in a safe, new home. Check with other recent home buyers if the house you are considering is one of several by the same builder. Perhaps a recent buyer has tested the sprayed ceiling finish, or you may find a neighbor who shares your concerns and offers to help defray the lab costs.

Most states have an office that deals with some or all of these environmental hazards. Call them if you have questions. Contact the following sources for additional information:

Environmental Protection Agency
Public Information Center
401 M Street, S.W.
Washington, D.C. 20460
Ask for documents on household asbestos, drinking water, lead, and radon.

U.S. Consumer Products Safety Commission
Office of Outreach Coordination
Washington, D.C. 20207
Document: *What You Should Know about Lead-Based Paint in Your House*

American Lung Association
1740 Broadway
New York, N.Y. 10019
Documents: *Air Pollution in Your Home, Home Indoor Air-Quality Checklist*

Consumer Federation of America
1424 16th Street, N.W.
Washington, D.C. 20036
Document: *Formaldehyde: Everything You Wanted to Know But Were Afraid to Ask*

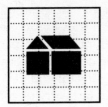

15

How to Make an Offer

Armed with your ability and the knowledge you have gained from this book, you should now have enough confidence to inspect a house for yourself. And you should be able to ask more knowledgeable questions of the seller or the agent you are dealing with. Remember, too, if you like your agent, stay with him or her. Some people think that only the agent whose name is on the "For Sale" sign can sell the house. This is generally not so. Respected agents cooperate. So even though one agent has the listing, he or she will usually allow others to sell the house.

Contrary to what some people say, an agent does perform many valuable services. He or she carefully selects houses for you to look at that suit your needs, thus saving you hours and days of useless running around by yourself. The agent has listings of what is on the market, with information on the number of rooms, baths, proximity to schools, class of neighborhood, zoning, taxes, appraised value, and so on. Another important agent service is arranging financing. This is important, for the agent has contact with lending agencies, and if he or she is well respected, the agency will often bend the rules and make a loan on a house that it might not consider otherwise. A good agent tries harder, for he or she needs the commission, arranges for termite inspections and any repairs needed, and acts as the negotiator between buyer and seller. He or she does the haggling for you. If you're not good at such confrontations, this can be a very uncomfortable experience. Some people enjoy it, but most do not. Know thyself!

Contracts

Writing a contract is perhaps the point of mystery most feared and respected by a buyer. Most people feel a lawyer is a necessity here. In some states an agent can write the contract, but this may not be wise if he or she is also working for, and being paid by, the seller. The contract gets the ball rolling, and that's what you want. The contract will name a title insurance company and an escrow agent to handle that business. Or you can name the companies you wish. And the contract will list all conditions of sale. If the contract is agreeable to both parties, the signatures are gathered, a deposit is made, and the agent or attorney then seeks financing. When that is approved, the contract goes to the escrow agent, where many details will be handled. When all conditions are satisfied, the escrow company will return the final papers to the agent and all of the details will be explained to the buyer and seller. The deal is then finalized.

But suppose you don't want to use an agent or lawyer; you want to buy directly from the seller. You're an adult, you can negotiate a loan. Once you and the seller come to an agreement, all you need is an escrow agent and perhaps a title insurance company. But before you open an escrow account, you've got to read the rest of this chapter, for there are many things you should know about the house. Here are a few of them.

You've already run yourself ragged and found the house you like; you're ready to start talking business. You've only walked through the house and have yet to make your inspection. But there are other facts and figures you should know about before you make your offer, in order to determine whether or not you can afford the costs of purchasing and maintaining the house.

1. How much are the taxes per year?
2. What is the tax rate per hundred assessed evaluation?
3. How much is the house assessed for?
4. When was it last assessed?
5. How much do utilities cost per month? Ask to see receipts.
6. How much will you have to borrow? Then ask a loan company how much the payments are per month on that amount, for twenty-five or thirty years at the going rate of interest. How much are closing costs?
7. How much is insurance?
8. What is the cost of upkeep? This is difficult to determine precisely, but there are always some repairs.

Assessed versus Appraised Values

After you've added up these figures, you're in a better position to know if you can afford the house.

There's a difference between assessed and appraised value. Assessed value is a percentage of appraised value, and the amount of that percentage varies from state to state and often from county to county, but the confusion is about the same. Appraised value is market value. Assessed value is taxation value. Your taxes are computed at so much per hundred assessed value. When you phone the assessor's office to learn the assessed value, ask what percentage that is of the appraised, or market value. Don't hesitate to call. This is public knowledge. They'll give it to you. Another thing to find out from local residents is whether there is a pending change in assessment policy, and how school taxes affect assessment. This could affect your tax bill substantially.

When you know what the house is assessed for, it is a good yardstick as to the value of the house. At least you know whether it is far overpriced. Assessors are supposed to assess at fair market value, but sometimes they are not up to date and prices can change quickly, depending upon the market in certain areas. Generally, houses do sell for more than the appraised value. The assessor's office may tell you the average percent of selling price over appraised value.

If, for example, you pay $80,000 for a house that is appraised for $60,000, your taxes will undoubtedly be increased within a year because the assessor will know what you paid; the market value went up. This will make a difference in your monthly costs. The law is changing in several states. Property taxes will simply be a certain percentage of the market value, plus adjustments for special districts.

Pest Reports

Ask the seller if he or she has had a termite inspection. If there is one, learn the date and whether the work was done. Ask to see the report. If the seller has no report, but you know the house was inspected in the last five years, in most states you can get a copy of the report for two dollars from the state pest control board. If you have a report, you can easily check it to see if the work has been done. If, on the other hand, the seller shows you a report of an inspection and a clearance, which is proof that the work has been done, and it was within the past two years, you can be quite certain the structure is free of infestation. If it was any longer ago than that, ask about doing an inspection now. The seller may say no.

Then it's up to you. If, after you have made your own inspection, you are not confident about the termite situation, you must decide whether you want to order a professional inspection. Some loan companies require a clearance before they will loan on a house. But even though the seller is not going to pay anything toward termite work, he or she will allow you to have an inspection if you pay for it. Ask around. In some states the rule is that the seller pays for a termite report and the results are negotiable. In others the buyer pays for the report and the seller does the work. Ordinarily it is not a case of law but of custom. The real estate boards in your area will tell you the normal procedure.

Public Files

Before you make an offer, go to the building and planning department. Ask if they have a file on the property. This is public knowledge also. Study the file. Anything you find is important; the file will show if building permits have been issued and finaled and what they were for. Sometimes the record shows when a roof was installed, or a water heater, deck, or second bath. In addition, it will tell you whether inspections were made on the room that was added to the house you want to buy. The seller may brag about the room, but was it done to code? Perhaps it was, but if no permit was issued, you know the building inspector didn't conduct all the required inspections.

You may find that all the facts on the file are favorable. In that case you'll have peace of mind. But check for the zoning classification for the area: single family, duplex, multiple? Learn what the sideyard setback requirements are, and determine if the house conforms to the ordinances. Mainly you want to learn if there are any restrictions, such as variances, that would make the house nonconforming. It could be a duplex, for example, but new zoning has made the area single family, R-1. In that case you would have a legal nonconforming use. That's not critical, but you should know it because any encumbrance makes the property harder to sell and makes it more difficult to get permission for improvements.

It's especially important to check with local officials if you plan to expand the house. Some communities require home-owners to pay for right-of-way improvements when they make additions. If the house is on a steep hillside, find out if the foundation was engineered, as most communities now require. You might even want to check with the fire department to see if it has any information about the house.

If blueprints are available, all the better. Examine them, but remember, the map is not the territory; blueprints don't guarantee that the house was built according to the plans.

All right, so no agent is involved. In this case the seller will undoubtedly know the procedure, but for your own protection you'd better be aware of how it's done. The seller has his or her interests; you have yours. Books have been written explaining how to sell your home without using an agent or broker, describing step by step what escrow agents and title insurance companies do for the seller and buyer, but actually their duties are so routine it's hardly worth a chapter. This is not to say they are not important; they have their place in our society. They are convenient and perform important jobs that are mysterious to most people. We have to live with them, so a brief explanation of their duties is in order.

Escrow

Escrow simply means a set of instructions given to a third party (escrow company) to hold your deposit until the conditions described in those instructions are met. For example: an escrow company will prorate taxes and fire insurance, see that the title is recorded for county records, pay off all trust deeds and mortgages, if any, withhold its fee, pay the title insurance company, etc. All of these disbursements will be explained to both buyer and seller, as mentioned.

Title Insurance

Title insurance is entirely different. The enduring nature of land makes it possible for several parties to claim rights to a piece of property. The claims could include an easement (right of way) across the land, an old judgment, an unpaid mortgage, a lien against the property, and many others. A title company makes a search of all available records to determine the soundness of the land title. If anything untoward is discovered, these findings will be revealed to you. In the event the title company feels there is clear title to the property, it will issue title insurance (for a fee) to protect you, the buyer, against title hazards. This insurance covers you for legal defense against an attack on a title by someone who believes that he has a claim to the property.

Very few states have a law making it mandatory that a buyer purchase title insurance. They don't force you to insure personal property from theft. It's up to you. But if you have to borrow money to buy the property, loan companies have a rule that you must insure the title. After all, it's really their house until the loan is paid off, and they want it insured, at your expense naturally. Skipping title insurance is generally not advisable. But ask what the costs are, then decide if the service and assurance are worth the price. There's nothing stopping you from making your own title search. County records are open to the public, so it is quite simple to search those records to learn if any mechanics' liens or encumbrances have been recorded. If you find none, and you feel absolutely safe that no heir can claim the property you wish to purchase, then skip the insurance, save the insurance costs, and buy the property.

The procedure for buying property without an agent differs from state to state, and sometimes within a state. In northern California, for example, most title insurance companies may also act as escrow agents if they are licensed to do so. In southern California the rule is that escrow companies are separate from title companies, but the trend is to combine them. Because rules vary from area to area and are also changing, it would be useless to describe what the procedure is now in the various states.

The best advice is to go to a title insurance company, or an escrow company, and tell them you are going to purchase a home without using an agent. Ask what the costs are and what the procedure is and tell them if you want them to handle it. They will be very helpful. It's their business to handle transactions like this.

But no matter what the procedure is in your particular area, it must be remembered that title insurance companies and escrow agents are disinterested third parties to any trans-action. That is, there must be total agreement between seller and buyer as to price and conditions before you go to the company to start proceedings for the final sale. They will not do any haggling for you.

In all probability, you will be told to get a "contract for the purchase of real estate and receipt of deposit." Easy. Almost all stationery stores carry this document, as do some title companies. You and the seller will get together and fill it out. At this time, you will make a deposit which will be returned to you if the conditions listed on the form are not met. And now we come to the most important part of your offer. Conditions.

For example: (1) The offer is subject to a house inspection by yourself or by a professional if you wish. (This clause will protect you if you find serious faults and the seller won't correct them or pay for them.) (2) Financing. You already know how much you have to borrow, so your offer could be subject to getting a loan of a certain amount on the house, at a certain rate of interest. These figures will be precise when you know them. (3) You may want the stove and the refrigerator, drapes, washer and dryer, carpets, chandeliers, mirrors; if so, make all these items a condition. (4) If you want a professional termite inspection, make that a condition. Sometimes the seller agrees to pay up to a certain amount toward termite work. If that is the case, be sure to state that amount in the agreement. (5) You may want assurance that all appliances will be kept in working order until the close of escrow. And to protect the seller, and give you some working time, you can stipulate that you will satisfy the conditions within ten or twenty days. Before you sign, you may want an attorney to check the papers. If you and the seller sign, you have a preliminary agreement and the house is off the market. Remember too that if you are purchasing through an agent, you can insist on the above conditions, and more if you think of them.

Now it's up to you to begin satisfying the conditions. Start with financing, for while the loaning institution is doing its work, you can be doing yours. Take this book with you and give the house a thorough inspection. When you get through, you'll know a lot more about the house than if you had taken an agent's word for it.

Suppose you find serious faults in the house, but you would still like to buy it. Show the faults to the seller and tell him you'll buy the house provided he does the repairs or has them done. Or, if you are handy and don't mind the work, tell the seller you'll purchase minus the amount you think it will cost to make repairs. And don't forget the termite report. If there is infestation, you'll have to come to an agreement with the seller. If the seller is adamant and won't cooperate, tell him or her you don't want the house and go find another one. But don't forget your deposit.

One thing is certain: it's better to lose a bad house because of your knowledge than to gain one through ignorance. Too many unwary buyers fall into the latter category.

If you have engaged an agent, and you or a private inspector have found serious faults on the property, the agent will then confront the seller with the facts. If you still like the house, you will ask that the faults be corrected or a sufficient amount of money be deducted to have them repaired. If the seller refuses to cooperate and makes a statement about selling to someone else instead, your agent must tell the seller that under the full disclosure law, which most states have, the agent must inform all prospective buyers about any known faults. It's a law to help consumers. The listing agent must be informed, and it would be fraudulent for the seller to withhold known information. Usually sellers cooperate, realizing they may as well cooperate with you as with someone else. And if the agent is firm in his convictions, he or she will reveal all known faults.

Back to the direct sale. When you and the seller agree that all conditions have been met, you will open escrow proceedings. Now there's very little chance the deal will not go through. When the time for closing of escrow has arrived, you and the seller will be notified and you and your attorneys, if hired, meet at the escrow company. It may be required that you have an attorney present. There all the figures and disbursements of money will be read and explained to you. If all is in order, the deed to the property will be signed over to you. You've bought yourself a house.

Your next step should be to consider homesteading your property. Most states allow this, and rightly so. In this country the tradition is that every person deserves a place to live. The law varies in different states, but essentially homesteading protects the homeowner from being wiped out completely by some calamity—a lawsuit, an illness, or some other misfortune. In California, for example, homestead exemptions apply up to $20,000 if you are married, $10,000 if you are single. This means that if a judgment is obtained against a homeowner over a lawsuit, an accident, medical costs, or the like, he or she would be protected for the amount listed. There are some exemptions, such as mechanics' liens and mortgages. If you don't make your payments, the mortgage company can foreclose and take your property, sell it, and keep what you owe them. But whatever is left over is protected from other creditors if your property is legally homesteaded.

The homestead law is very lenient "way out west," but they can afford it. Most states do very little for homesteading. Check it out. The county clerk knows about it, or ask an attorney. You may find that you can get a form for homesteading in a stationery store, fill it out, have it notarized, and for a small fee have it recorded in the county records. It makes a lot of sense to look into homesteading. After all, laws are made to be used, not abused.

16

Your
Semiannual
Maintenance
Schedule

Keeping your house in shape is simply a matter of paying attention to problems and fixing them before they get out of control. Spending just an hour or two inspecting your home each spring and fall will keep you from having to make expensive repairs in summer and winter.

When making these inspections, having a checklist will keep you from overlooking some simple but potentially costly problems. By using the simple checklist that follows (and healing the wounds of your aging home as quickly as possible), you can add years of life to your house and save hundreds of dollars on repairs and possibly thousands of dollars in replacement costs.

The Fall Maintenance Schedule

When doing seasonal maintenance inspections, bear in mind that your task is twofold. First, you are inspecting for damage and wear and tear from the previous season. Second, you are preparing the house for the coming season. In all seasons you'll want to give the house a quick inspection from foundation to roof just to check for problems.

Fall is the time to batten down the hatches. You want to make sure your house is ready for the coming cold. Start in your basement or cellar and work your way up through the house. Pay particular attention to your gutters—they'll need cleaning.

Interior

Begin by inspecting both the interior and exterior foundation for cracks or voids. These are an open invitation for excess water as well as rodents and insects. Should you see any signs of moisture, you have reason to suspect a leak in the foundation. Be sure to patch any of the cracks or holes that you find.

While you are downstairs, give your heating system the once-over. If you have a steam heating system, this means bringing up the level of water. If you use oil, you should check your fuel supply and clean your furnace air filters.

At this time you should be tightening up around windows and doors to prevent unnecessary heat loss. Check your entry doors and storm doors to make sure they are operating properly and are weathertight. Check to see that your windows and storm windows are not cracked. Then replace all your screen windows and doors with storm windows and doors. If your windows have sash cords, look to see that they are not broken. Be sure that the putty seal surrounding the windows is intact.

Fall Maintenance Schedule: Interior

- ☐ Patch cracks in foundation.
- ☐ Check dryness.
- ☐ Test furnace (schedule a tune-up).
- ☐ Replace or clean air filters in furnace.
- ☐ Check all fluid levels of heating system.
  - Water level ☐ empty ☐ half ☐ full
  - Oil level ☐ empty ☐ half ☐ full
- ☐ Insulate basement windows.
- ☐ Replace screen windows and doors with storm windows and doors.
- ☐ Check all windows for cracks.
- ☐ Check sash cords.
- ☐ Check putty seal.
- ☐ Make sure all doors are working properly.
- ☐ Make sure all windows and doors are weathertight.

Exterior

No matter what climate you live in, fall is an ideal time of year to do exterior painting. The humidity is low, the temperature is bearable, and rainfall is only intermittent. It is also a good time to check your gutters. All gutters should be cleaned thoroughly. If your gutters are made of wood, be sure to oil them as well. The oil will preserve the wood and will prevent them from clogging. It will also deter the eventual backflow of rainwater and the possibility of ice damming up under the roof shingles. Aluminum gutters should be checked for rust buildup.

While you are cleaning the gutters, check the condition of the roof. It is important to do this well before the colder and wetter months set in, as any necessary repairs must be done before the bad weather. Check to see that the shingles are holding strong and that there are no cracks, holes, or soft spots.

Remember to check the exterior foundation for cracks and voids.

Fall Maintenance Schedule: Exterior

☐ Do any exterior painting or staining that is necessary.
☐ Clean and oil gutters when necessary.
☐ Check the roof.
☐ Check the foundation for cracks and voids.

The Spring Maintenance Schedule

If fall is the time to batten down for the cold, spring is the time to prepare for the coming summer. You will notice that many of the maintenance procedures are similar to those done in the fall—cleaning the gutters and heating system, for example. Yet, in some instances, you actually will have to "undo" what you did in the fall.

Interior
Again, begin in the basement. You should reexamine the foundation as cracks or voids may develop as a result of a particularly cold or stormy winter. Examine your plumbing system as well to make sure there are no leaks. While you are still in the basement, take time to clean your heating unit. If your heating system is run on steam, this is the time of year it must be drained.

Before replacing your storm windows and doors with

screens, be certain to check them thoroughly. Make sure there are no cracks in the windows and no caulking problems. Lubricate all metal hinges and clasps around the windows and doors (and cupboards as well). You might want to soap the window edges and sashes to ease movement of the window.

The availability of fresh air makes this a good time for interior painting, papering, or floor refinishing. The breezes can diffuse the otherwise toxic fumes.

For those of you with a fireplace, this is the time of year to have a professional chimney sweep clean your chimney. You can help by cleaning the fireplace itself.

Spring Maintenance Schedule: Interior

☐ Patch cracks in foundation.
☐ Check dryness.
☐ Make sure there are no leaks in the plumbing.
☐ Clean or drain the heating system.
☐ Replace the storm windows and doors with screen windows and doors.
☐ Check windows and caulking for cracks.
☐ Lubricate all metal hinges and clasps.
☐ Do any necessary interior painting, papering, or refinishing.
☐ Clean chimney and fireplace.

Exterior

Spring is the time to think about the exterior of your home. For example, are you considering doing any landscaping or gardening? Soil is soft in the spring, and new gardens can be dug very easily. You also may need to do some pruning where the winter's winds have torn down branches and the like.

Carefully check your porch and railings for dry rot or

excessive wear. While walking around the outside of your house, make sure that your downspouts are in place and that none are missing. Once again, check to see that your gutters are clean. You should go up to the roof to see that no twigs or branches have fallen into the gutters. Also, carefully examine the roof. Make sure that there are no holes or leaks or soft spots. Finally, take a look at the siding on the house. Determine whether you will need to do any repainting, staining, or siding before the next winter.

Spring Maintenance Schedule: Exterior

☐ Check exterior foundation for cracks or voids.
☐ Plan and prepare ground for landscaping or gardening.
☐ Clear away all branches or twigs thrown about in winter storms.
☐ Check porch and railings for dry rot and wear.
☐ See that the roof is in good condition.
☐ Clean gutters.
☐ Check exterior siding.

Appendix A

Condominiums

....

In general this book applies to all kinds of buildings, whether single family or multiple. But because condominiums have grown in popularity, a few words of caution to people seeking that type of housing are in order. Group living makes sense in areas where land values are high, but we all need privacy to keep our senses.

Aside from the overall construction of the building, the single most important aspect of condominium living is soundproofing. If the building is fifteen years old or more, be very careful about checking into sound. Light classical music doesn't mix well with hard rock. Spend some time in the apartment while occupants are home, both alongside and overhead. Listen carefully for sounds in water pipes, steps overhead, doors closing, stereos, and street traffic. The last is important, especially for night ventilation, so open a window and listen for street noises.

The newer buildings have double-wall construction, and insulation is almost always used, so sounds seldom come through walls from adjoining apartments. But it is much harder to insulate between floors, so pay attention to that important detail.

Following are some other points to consider while shopping for group living.

☐ *Heating:* If there is central heat, do you have positive individual control? You don't want to be governed by someone else's idea of comfort. How is the cost divided? And who pays for upkeep and cost of repair? Forced-air furnaces are common, and some of them are noisy. If there's a furnace for each unit, turn it on and check for noise. Some of them emit a whoosh of air that continues all the time the fan is on. The fan noise can be distracting.

☐ *Plumbing:* Are there individual water heaters or is there a general source that is supposed to provide enough hot water to go around? If from a general source, who pays costs and upkeep? Are costs shared equally regardless of family size? If there are two of you and families of four in other units, that's a consideration. How is general maintenance handled?

☐ **Parking:** How is the security for all-night parking? What arrangements are there for guests, yours and others? Are cars starting their motors and testing their carburetors early in the morning going to bother you?

☐ **Security:** Is there good lighting from the parking area to your door? Are corridors well lighted?

☐ **Fire:** Are there fire extinguishers and smoke detectors in hallways and corridors? Better have smoke detectors in your own unit also.

☐ **Swimming guests:** Can you invite all the friends you wish to come and swim? If so, remember that other owners have the same privilege. Think about it.

☐ **Decks:** Concrete decks over wood often are troublesome. Concrete is not waterproof. There must be a good waterproofing agent between the concrete and the wood beneath. You can't see it, so try to get beneath the deck and look for water stains. If you see any, beware. It could mean wood rot. Perhaps the owner will take care of it, but it is best to avoid buying trouble.

☐ **Repairs:** You are responsible for your own apartment, but what if, for example, a plumbing leak from above occurs? Your ceiling is ruined. Whose responsibility is it and who pays for your repair? Is it entirely up to you to take care of the problem?

Besides the physical aspects mentioned, it cannot be stressed too much that you must thoroughly understand the legal document you sign; it should clearly specify your commitment and also the association's responsibilities. Read and keep a copy of the condominium association's conditions, covenants, and rules. If you are in any doubt about even the smallest detail, ask questions and understand the answers. Or engage an attorney to check it.

Is there a management firm that takes care of the grounds, pool, and other general maintenance? Do you have a vote in the management policy? Ask about an owners' association, and if there is one, learn how it functions. Ask to see its financial statements. Proper management sets aside large financial reserves for upkeep and improvements of the common areas. Generally speaking, the larger the association the smaller your voice. Leave nothing to chance. Simply keep in mind that this will be your home, your shelter. Don't be a victim of those famous last words after it's too late: "You signed the agreement."

Appendix B

Inspection Checklist

....

The following checklist is a valuable tool not only for buyers but also for homeowners. The procedures are structured so as to take you through a house in the same thorough and efficient manner that professional home inspectors use. The more complex features whose function affects the house as a whole are listed separately for your convenience.

Some of the questions below that concern health hazards can be definitely answered only by a professional, and with the permission of the homeowner. Do not try to take asbestos samples yourself, as this may release fibers into the air. If what you see does not rule out a health hazard, place a question mark next to it. When you're done, look back and decide whether you want a professional to inspect the house more thoroughly.

Please note that questions marked by an asterisk are ones that may not be necessary to ask in every climate.

Before you begin the actual inspection, be sure to make note of the following items.

	Yes	No
What type of **fuel** is used? _____		
What is the approximate **age** of the house? _____		
Approximately how much fuel will be used during the colder months? $_____ units _____		
Does this include cooking?	☐	☐
Use of the water heater?	☐	☐

Exterior

	Yes	No
What is the **exterior?**		
☐ paint ☐ stain ☐ siding ☐ stone ☐ cement ☐ other		
What is the condition of the exterior?		
☐ cracking ☐ checking ☐ peeling		
Does the paint contain **lead?**	☐	☐
What is the **siding** made of?		
☐ vinyl ☐ aluminum		
Does the siding contain **asbestos?**	☐	☐
Is the siding firm? ☐ loose? ☐		
Will you need to replace it?	☐	☐
Do you plan to add to the house?	☐	☐
In what condition is the **window trim?**		
☐ good ☐ fair ☐ poor		
Will you need to scrape and paint it?	☐	☐
Will you need to replace it?	☐	☐
Is the **putty** serviceable?	☐	☐
Is it cracked?	☐	☐
Does it need replacing?	☐	☐
Is the **caulking** serviceable?	☐	☐
Check the **molding** in all corners, doorways, and windows.		
Does any of it need renailing?	☐	☐
If so, where? _____		
Does any of it need replacement?	☐	☐
If so, where? _____		
What are the conditions of the **chimneys** and **vents?**		
☐ good ☐ fair ☐ poor		
Do the chimneys have **spark arresters?**	☐	☐
Are the **stairs** in good condition?		
☐ good ☐ fair ☐ poor		
Do they have **handrails?**	☐	☐
Are they illuminated?	☐	☐

Drainage

	Yes	No

What are the **gutters** made of?
wood _____ galvanized sheet metal _____
If they are wood, when was the last time they were oiled?

_____

	Yes	No
If they are metal, are they rusty?	☐	☐
Are the gutters clear and clean?	☐	☐
Will you need to replace them?	☐	☐
Are there any **downspouts?**	☐	☐

What condition are they in?
☐ good ☐ rusty
Where do they drain into? _____

	Yes	No
Does the water flow *away* from the house?	☐	☐
Or does the water settle into the foundation?	☐	☐
Is there a **leader drain?**	☐	☐

What condition is it in?
☐ good ☐ rusty

Roof

What kind of **roof** is it?
☐ tar-and-gravel ☐ wood shingles ☐ shakes
☐ metal ☐ asphalt shingles ☐ slate ☐ other
What condition is the roof in?
☐ good ☐ fair ☐ poor
If the neighbor's roof is the same age, what is its condition?
☐ original ☐ replacement _____ (when? _____)
☐ good ☐ fair ☐ poor
What condition are the **ridges** in?
☐ good ☐ fair ☐ poor
What condition are the **valleys** in?
☐ good ☐ fair ☐ poor
What conditions are the **flashings** in?
☐ good ☐ fair ☐ poor

	Yes	No

What condition are the roof **tiles** in?
□ good □ missing tiles □ turned-up tiles

	Yes	No
*Are there **snow guards**?	□	□
*Is there an **ice dam barrier**?	□	□

Attic Area

	Yes	No
Is there any evidence of roof **leaks**?	□	□
Is the attic properly **ventilated**?	□	□
Is the attic **insulated**?	□	□
Is it accessible to insulate:	□	□

What size are the **roof rafters**? _____

	Yes	No
Are the rafters properly spaced?	□	□
Is there any evidence of **sagging**?	□	□
Are there **collar beams** (bracing)?	□	□
Is there a **knee wall**?	□	□
Are the **floor joists** spaced properly?	□	□

What is the length of the span between the **bearing walls**?

_____

	Yes	No
Is there any evidence of sagging here?	□	□

Is there **flooring material**?
□ yes □ no □ partial

	Yes	No
*Is there evidence of the existence of **ice dams**?	□	□
*Are there **hurricane ties**?	□	□

Electric

What is the service size in **amperes**? _____
How many **circuits** are there? _____
What is the **voltage**?
□ 230 □ 115 □ other

	Yes	No
Is there a **main disconnect**?	□	□

How many **circuit breakers** are there? _____

	Yes	No
Are they properly identified?	□	□

	Yes	No
How many **fuses** are there? _____		
Are they properly identified?	☐	☐
Are the circuits overfused?	☐	☐
Is the **wiring** neat?	☐	☐
Is the wiring **grounded?**	☐	☐
Are there appliance circuits in the kitchen?	☐	☐
Is the wiring adequate?	☐	☐
Will you need to do rewiring?	☐	☐
Partial rewiring?	☐	☐
Are there 230-volt outlets?	☐	☐

Heating

What type of **heating system** does the house have?
☐ forced-air ☐ gravity ☐ electric ☐ hot water
☐ radiant ☐ oil ☐ gas ☐ other

	Yes	No
Do the heating **controls** work?	☐	☐
Is the **combustion chamber** clean?	☐	☐
Will the heating unit need cleaning to improve efficiency?	☐	☐
What is the number of **BTUs?**_____		
If the heating unit is forced-air, is the motor unit clean?	☐	☐
Will it be easy to change the filter?	☐	☐
Has the **heat exchanger** been tested?	☐	☐
Do any uninsulated **heating ducts** exist in unheated spaces?	☐	☐
Does the duct insulation contain **asbestos** fibers?	☐	☐
Is there adequate **combustion venting?**	☐	☐
Are the **radiators** and **valves** working properly?	☐	☐

Plumbing

	Yes	No
Is there **copper** tubing? _____		
Galvanized **steel?** _____		
Have you made sure the pipes are *not* made of **lead?**	☐	☐
If the pipes are of galvanized steel, how old are they? _____		

	Yes	No

How are galvanized pipes connected to copper pipes?
 ☐ dielectric fittings ☐ brass fittings

Are copper pipes connected with lead solder?   ☐ ☐

Do the water pipes have **shut-off valves** in the
 ☐ basement? ☐ kitchen? ☐ bathroom?

Do the **waste pipes** have leaks in them?   ☐ ☐
Are the **clean-out plugs** accessible?   ☐ ☐
 Are the waste pipes clean?   ☐ ☐
 Do they have any leaks in them?   ☐ ☐
Do you anticipate many plumbing repairs?   ☐ ☐

What is the source of **drinking water?**
 ☐ municipal system ☐ domestic well

Where does **sewage** go?
 ☐ municipal system ☐ septic tank

Water Heater

Is the water heater **gas** or **electric?**
 ☐ gas ☐ electric

What is its **gallon capacity?** _____

Is there a **temperature relief valve?**   ☐ ☐
Is there a proper **flue?**   ☐ ☐
Is there a proper **gas supply pipe?**   ☐ ☐
Does the heater have adequate **ventilation?**   ☐ ☐
If there is a gas heater in the garage, is it up off the floor?   ☐ ☐

Crawl Space and Foundation

Are there any signs of **moisture?**   ☐ ☐

How is the **wood-to-soil clearance?**
 ☐ good ☐ fair ☐ poor

Is there any evidence of **dry rot?**   ☐ ☐
Is there adequate **underfloor ventilation?**   ☐ ☐
Are there any signs of **termites** or **rodents?**   ☐ ☐
Is the foundation made of continuous concrete?   ☐ ☐

	Yes	**No**
Are there **cracks** in the foundation?	☐	☐
Are they severe or are they hairline cracks? _____		
Are there **piers?**	☐	☐
Are the piers firm?	☐	☐
Are the **girders** sagging?	☐	☐
Are the posts spaced correctly?	☐	☐
Are the **posts** plumb?	☐	☐
What is the size of the **floor joists?**_____		
What is their span?_____		
Are they spaced properly?	☐	☐
Is there any evidence of a **sagging** floor?	☐	☐
Is there **bridging** between the joists?	☐	☐
What is the **subfloor** made of? _____		

Kitchen

What is the **ceiling** made of?
  ☐ plaster ☐ gypsum board ☐ plywood
  ☐ sprayed finish containing asbestos ☐ other
  Is the ceiling painted? ☐
  ☐ wallpapered?

	Yes	No
Is there any evidence of cracks?	☐	☐
Is there any evidence of a leak?	☐	☐

What are the **walls** made of?
  ☐ plaster ☐ gypsum board ☐ tile ☐ paneling ☐ other
  Are they painted? ☐ wallpapered? ☐

	Yes	No
Is there any evidence of cracking?	☐	☐

What is the **floor** made of?
  ☐ wood ☐ vinyl ☐ linoleum ☐ tiles that contain asbestos

	Yes	No
Is it carpeted?	☐	☐
Is it insulated?	☐	☐

  What condition is the floor in?
  ☐ good ☐ fair ☐ poor

	Yes	No
Do you detect a slope in the floor?	☐	☐

	Yes	No

How many **windows** are there? _____

Are they double-hung windows? ☐ ☐

What is the **sash** made of?

☐ wood ☐ metal ☐ other

Are the **frames** in good condition? ☐ ☐

Are they rotted? ☐ ☐

Are they cracked? ☐ ☐

Are they loose? ☐ ☐

Are they weather-stripped? ☐ ☐

Are the **cords** broken? ☐ ☐

Are the **sills** in good condition? ☐ ☐

Are they rotted? ☐ ☐

Do they show any evidence of air leaks? ☐ ☐

Are there **storm windows?** ☐ ☐

Are there **screens?** ☐ ☐

What is the cost estimate for **plastic sheeting?** _____

Is the **hardware** (locks, knobs, latches, etc.) in good condition? ☐ ☐

Will certain items need replacing? ☐ ☐

How many?_____

Are the **doors** in good condition? ☐ ☐

Do they fit tightly? ☐ ☐

Are they weather-stripped? ☐ ☐

Do they scrape the floor? ☐ ☐

Do they close properly? ☐ ☐

Is the doorsill flush? ☐ ☐

Are there storm doors? ☐ ☐

Are there screen doors? ☐ ☐

Are the **plumbing fixtures** in good condition? ☐ ☐

Will they need replacement? ☐ ☐

Does the faucet drip? ☐ ☐

How is the **water pressure?**

☐ strong ☐ weak

Are there **valves** beneath the sink? ☐ ☐

Do they leak? ☐ ☐

Are there **P trap** leaks? ☐ ☐

Is there a **garbage disposal?** ☐ ☐

Does it work? ☐ ☐

What is the **sink** made of?

☐ stainless steel ☐ cast-iron, white ☐ steel, white

	Yes	No
Is it chipped?	☐	☐
Is it crazed?	☐	☐
Will the sink need replacing?	☐	☐

What are the **countertops** made of?
☐ Formica ☐ tile ☐ wood ☐ other
What condition are they in?
☐ good ☐ fair ☐ poor

	Yes	No
Is there enough **cabinet space**?	☐	☐
Are there enough electrical **outlets?**	☐	☐
Are the outlets GFCI-protected?	☐	☐

What size **wires** are being used?
☐ #12 ☐ #14

	Yes	No
Are they individually grounded?	☐	☐

What condition are the **light fixtures** in?
☐ good ☐ fair ☐ poor

	Yes	No
Will they need replacing?	☐	☐

What kind of **stove** will come with the house?
☐ gas ☐ electric ☐ none
What condition is it in?
☐ good ☐ fair ☐ poor

	Yes	No
Will it need replacing?	☐	☐
Is there an exhaust fan?	☐	☐
Will a **refrigerator** come with the house?	☐	☐
If so, is it in operating condition?	☐	☐
Is it plumbed for an ice maker?	☐	☐

Bathroom

What is the **ceiling** made of?
☐ plaster ☐ gypsum board ☐ sprayed finish
containing asbestos ☐ other
Is the ceiling painted? ☐ wallpapered? ☐

	Yes	No
Are there any cracks in the ceiling?	☐	☐
Is there any evidence of a leak?	☐	☐

What are the **walls** made of?
☐ plaster ☐ gypsum board ☐ tile ☐ paneling
Are they painted? ☐ wallpapered? ☐

	Yes	No

What condition are the walls in?
□ good □ fair □ poor
What is the **floor** made of?
□ tile □ linoleum □ vinyl □ asphalt tile

	Yes	No
Do the tiles contain asbestos?	□	□
Is it insulated?	□	□

What condition is the floor in?
□ good □ fair □ poor

Is there an individual **shower**?	□	□
Or is the shower in the tub?	□	□

What is the **shower wall** made of?
□ Formica □ tile □ wallboard □ other
What condition are the walls in?
□ good □ fair □ poor
If the wall is tiled, what is it tiled with?
□ **mortar** □ **mastic**

Are the tiles firm?	□	□
Is a soapdish part of the tiles?	□	□

What condition is the soapdish in?
□ loose □ watertight
What condition is the **grout** in?
□ good □ fair □ poor
How is the **water pressure?**
□ good □ fair □ poor
What is the **lavatory counter** made of?
□ tile □ Formica □ other
What condition is it in?
□ good □ fair □ poor

Is the **toilet seal** firm?	□	□
Or can you detect a leak?	□	□

Is the **tub** chipped? □ crazed? □ serviceable? □
Are the **fixtures** modern? □ old? □ serviceable? □

Does the **faucet** have a drip?	□	□
Are there any **P trap** leaks?	□	□
Are there any **valve** leaks?	□	□
Is there adequate **ventilation?**	□	□

Living Room

	Yes	No
What is the **ceiling** made of?		
☐ plaster ☐ gypsum board ☐ Celotex ☐ panels		
☐ sprayed finish containing asbestos ☐ other		
Is the ceiling painted? ☐ wallpapered? ☐		
Are there cracks in the ceiling?	☐	☐
Is there evidence of leaks?	☐	☐
What are the **walls** made of?		
☐ plaster ☐ gypsum board ☐ paneling ☐ other		
Are they painted? ☐ wallpapered? ☐		
Are there any cracks in the walls?	☐	☐
What is the **floor** made of?		
☐ hardwood ☐ fir ☐ asphalt tile		
☐ tiles that contain asbestos ☐ other		
Is it carpeted?	☐	☐
Is it insulated?	☐	☐
What condition is the floor in?		
☐ good ☐ fair ☐ poor		
Is there a slope to the floor?	☐	☐
Do the **doors** fit properly?	☐	☐
Are the **locks** on the doors secure?	☐	☐
Are the doors weather-stripped?	☐	☐
Is the doorsill flush?	☐	☐
How many **windows** are there? _____		
Are they double-hung?	☐	☐
Are the windows framed in wood? ☐ metal? ☐ other? ☐		
Are any windows cracked?	☐	☐
Are the **frames** rotted?	☐	☐
Are there any leaks?	☐	☐
Are the windows weather-stripped?	☐	☐
Are the **cords** broken?	☐	☐
Are the **sills** rotted?	☐	☐
Are there any air leaks in the sills?	☐	☐
Are there **storm windows?**	☐	☐
Are there **screens?**	☐	☐
What is the cost estimate for **plastic sheeting?** _____		

	Yes	No

What is the **sash** made of?
☐ aluminum ☐ wood

Is there any evidence of **leakage**? ☐ ☐

Is the **hardware** in good condition? ☐ ☐

Will certain items need replacing? ☐ ☐

How many? _____

If there is a **wood stove,** has the owner shown you a permit? ☐ ☐

If there is a **fireplace,** how will it be equipped?
☐ damper ☐ screen ☐ spark arrester ☐ andirons
☐ fire tongs

Is the **hearth** free of cracks? ☐ ☐

What is the condition of the **bricks?**
☐ good ☐ fair ☐ poor

Is the **grout** firm? ☐ ☐

Is the **mantel** level? ☐ ☐

Is there any evidence of **smoke?** ☐ ☐

Smoke Detectors

How many **smoke detectors** are there? _____

Are they working properly? ☐ ☐

Are they properly located (near bedrooms, in the hallways, etc.)? ☐ ☐

Have they been placed too close to areas prone to harmless smoke (stoves, laundry rooms)? ☐ ☐

Family Room

What is the **ceiling** made of?
☐ plaster ☐ gypsum board ☐ Celotex ☐ panels
☐ sprayed finish containing asbestos ☐ other

Is the ceiling painted? ☐ wallpapered? ☐

Are there cracks in the ceiling? ☐ ☐

Is there any evidence of leaks? ☐ ☐

	Yes	No
What are the **walls** made of?		
☐ plaster ☐ gypsum board ☐ paneling ☐ other		
Are they painted? ☐ wallpapered? ☐		
Are there any cracks in the walls?	☐	☐
What is the **floor** made of?		
☐ hardwood ☐ fir ☐ asphalt tile		
☐ tiles that contain asbestos ☐ other		
Is it carpeted?	☐	☐
Is it insulated?	☐	☐
What condition is the floor in?		
☐ good ☐ fair ☐ poor		
Is there a slope to the floor?	☐	☐
Do the **doors** fit properly?	☐	☐
Are the locks on the doors secure?	☐	☐
Are the doors weather-stripped?	☐	☐
Is the doorsill flush?	☐	☐
How many **windows** are there? _____		
Are the windows framed in wood? ☐ metal? ☐ other? ☐		
Are any windows cracked?	☐	☐
Are the **frames** rotted?	☐	☐
Are there any air leaks?	☐	☐
Are the windows weather-stripped?	☐	☐
Are the **cords** broken?	☐	☐
Are the **sills** rotted?	☐	☐
Are there any air leaks in the **sills?**	☐	☐
Are there **storm windows?**	☐	☐
Are there **screens?**	☐	☐
What is the cost estimate for **plastic sheeting?** _____		
What is the **sash** made of?		
☐ aluminum ☐ wood		
Is there any evidence of **leakage?**	☐	☐
If there is a wood stove, has the owner shown you a permit?	☐	☐
Is the **hardware** in good condition?	☐	☐
Will certain items need replacing?	☐	☐
How many? _____		
If there is a **fireplace,** how will it be equipped?		
☐ damper ☐ screen ☐ spark arrester ☐ andirons		
☐ fire tongs		
Is the **hearth** free of cracks?	☐	☐

	Yes	No

What is the condition of the **bricks?**
  ☐ good ☐ fair ☐ poor
Is the **grout** firm? ☐ ☐
Is the **mantel** level? ☐ ☐
Is there any evidence of **smoke?** ☐ ☐
How many **heat registers** are there? _____
How many **electric outlets** are there? _____

Bedroom

What is the **ceiling** made of?
  ☐ plaster ☐ gypsum board ☐ Celotex ☐ panels
  ☐ sprayed finish containing asbestos ☐ other
  Is the ceiling painted? ☐ wallpapered? ☐
  Are there cracks in the ceiling? ☐ ☐
  Is there any evidence of leaks? ☐ ☐
What are the **walls** made of?
  ☐ plaster ☐ gypsum board ☐ paneling ☐ other
  Are they painted? ☐ wallpapered? ☐
  Are there any cracks in the walls? ☐ ☐
What is the **floor** made of?
  ☐ hardwood ☐ fir ☐ asphalt tile
  ☐ tiles that contain asbestos ☐ other
  What condition is the floor in?
  ☐ good ☐ fair ☐ poor
Is there a slope to the floor? ☐ ☐
Do the **doors** fit properly? ☐ ☐
  Are the **locks** on the door secure? ☐ ☐
  Are the doors weather-stripped? ☐ ☐
  Is the doorsill flush? ☐ ☐
How many **windows** are there? _____
  Are they double-hung? ☐ ☐
  Are the **windows** framed in wood? ☐ metal? ☐ other? ☐
  Are any windows cracked? ☐ ☐
  Are the **frames** rotted? ☐ ☐
  Are there any air leaks? ☐ ☐
  Are the windows weather-stripped? ☐ ☐

	Yes	No
Are the **cords** broken?	☐	☐
Are the **sills** rotted?	☐	☐
Are there any air leaks in the **sills?**	☐	☐
Are there **storm windows?**	☐	☐
Are there **screens?**	☐	☐

What is the cost estimate for **plastic sheeting?** _____

What is the **sash** made of?
☐ aluminum ☐ wood

	Yes	No
Is there any evidence of **leakage?**	☐	☐
Is the hardware in good condition?	☐	☐
Will certain items need replacing?	☐	☐

How many? _____

Would the windows allow people to **escape** if there is a fire? ☐ ☐

If there is a **fireplace,** how will it be equipped?
☐ damper ☐ screen ☐ spark arrester ☐ andirons
☐ fire tongs

Is the **hearth** free of cracks? ☐ ☐

What is the condition of the **bricks?**
☐ good ☐ fair ☐ poor

	Yes	No
Is the **grout** firm?	☐	☐
Is the **mantel** level?	☐	☐
Is there any evidence of **smoke?**	☐	☐

How many **heat registers** are there? _____

How many **electric outlets** are there? _____

Laundry

Is the house equipped for a **clothes dryer?** ☐ ☐
☐ gas outlet ☐ 230-volt electric receptacle

Environmental Hazards

Have the owners had the house **tested** for any hazards?
☐ radon ☐ formaldehyde ☐ lead paint ☐ asbestos ☐ other

	Yes	No
Have you seen the test results?	☐	☐

Have the owners provided complete **maintenance** records?
☐ water well ☐ septic system ☐ other

Did you notice household **chemicals** which should be removed by the buyer?	☐	☐
Was the soil or garage floor stained with **motor oil?**	☐	☐
Is the house located near existing or pre-existing environmental hazards?	☐	☐
Are there sources of **pollution** in the neighborhood?	☐	☐

☐ highways ☐ old factories ☐ old dumps ☐ gas stations
☐ other

Municipal Building Department

Is the file for this house complete?	☐	☐
Does the file contain any possible warnings?		

☐ permits without followup inspections ☐ citations
☐ restrictions on expansion ☐ other

Glossary

Amp   Ampere. Measure of electricity. Equal to the movement of 6.28 quintillion electrons per second. See *volt* and *watt*.
Angle of repose   Poetic but accurate phrase. The slope at which the earth is at rest. Natural slope.
Angle stop valve   Shut-off valves beneath sinks, lavatories, and toilets.
Appraised value   Market value. An amount the assessor thinks the property is worth.
Arcing   When screws holding aluminum wiring to terminals in the service panel become loose—a common tendency with aluminum wiring—electricity "arcs" across space. Can cause fires.
Asbestos   A fibrous mineral found in rocks and soil. Good for insulating, but inhaling its microscopic fibers is known to contribute to serious diseases. Today asbestos is almost entirely banned from new products, but it's still present in some older houses.
Asphalt-fiberglass shingles   New roofing material that is relatively thin, light, and very durable; lasts twenty to forty years in hot climates.
Asphalt shingles   Very common roofing material; available in a wide variety of grades, colors, and weights. Also known as composition shingles.
Assessed value   A percentage of appraised value for tax purposes. It's confusing, and meant to be. If it were clear, the common people could understand it. The tax rate is a certain amount for each one hundred dollars of assessed value.

Beam   See *girder*.
Bearing wall   Supports a floor above, or a portion of the roof. See *curtain wall*.
Blistering   Film of paint separated from its surface. Usually caused by moisture in the wood.

Bonnet packing   Pliable material around a valve stem to prevent water from leaking around the handle. If you can't find the right size packing, use cotton string.

BTU   British thermal unit. Amount of heat required to raise the temperature of a pound of water one degree Fahrenheit. Very close to the amount of heat from a wooden kitchen match.

Built-up roof   Same as tar-and-gravel roof. Several layers of thin tar paper with hot tar between courses, gravel on top.

Buttress   A support projecting from a wall.

Butyl   A plastic caulking compound.

Calignum   Liquid plastic used to fill the pores of deteriorated wood, especially rotted areas. Excellent for minor wood rot around windows. Other brand names: Git-Rot, Rot-Cure.

Carpenter ants   Large ants that live in hollowed spaces in wood. More a nuisance than a destroyer. Cleanliness is the answer.

Carpenter bees   Large black-and-yellow insects that look like bumblebees but are different. Leave galleries of ½-inch holes in wood.

Casing   The wooden boards of various widths on the walls outlining windows and doors.

Cats   Usually two-by-fours nailed between studs halfway between floor and ceiling. See *fire stop*.

Caulking   Any substance used to fill cracks.

Cellulose debris   Wood scraps lying on the earth beneath a house and not attached to the structure. Termite inspectors' favorite phrase to mystify homeowners, this is not a serious house disease.

Cement   A fine powder made from limestone, shale, marl, gypsum, and other rock products. These materials are fired in a large kiln, then ground to a gray powder. That's cement. When mixed with water, sand, and rocks, it becomes concrete.

Centrally located   To what? A football stadium, an auditorium, a cemetery? A suspect real estate term.

Chalking   Powdering of oil-based paint after a few years. It's a self-cleaning process to be expected.

Checking   Paint film that looks like alligator hide. Generally caused by poor primer.

Cheerful   Real estate term. Probably means that the seller is going to be laughing all the way to the bank.

Circuit   A complete path of electric current through several outlets, lights, or switches and returning to the source, which is the fuse box or circuit breaker box.

Circuit breaker Safety device to interrupt a circuit. It takes the place of the fuse, which was just as good.

Circuit-breaker panel See *service panel.*

Clean-out Plug or cap in sewer line easily removed to clean the pipe when necessary.

Clearance Report by a pest control inspector that a house is free of wood-destroying organisms and meets pest control specifications. Sometimes called a certificate.

Closing costs A charge based on percentage of the loan. Please pay the loan company.

Cold-air return Large ducts that lead cold air, or return air, to a furnace. Absolutely necessary.

Collar beam Beam, usually made of wood, used to connect opposite rafters together. Sometimes called straining piece.

Combustion venting Necessary fresh air leading to an oil- or gas-burning appliance. Without fresh air, the flame burns less efficiently. Same as oxygen venting.

Composition shingles See *Asphalt shingles.*

Concrete A mixture of cement, sand, water, and rocks.

Condensation Moisture forming on a cold surface where warmer air strikes. Windows and metal sash make good conditions for condensation. See *dew point.*

Conductor Wires that conduct electricity.

Contingency Dependent on something, a condition. For instance, you make an offer contingent upon a favorable inspection.

Crawl space The area between the earth and the floor. Not the most inviting area but an important one. Get acquainted with it.

Creosote Dangerous soot created by burning freshly cut wood rather than seasoned wood. Can build up to dangerous levels in wood stove or fireplace flues.

Cricket A built-up structure, six or eight inches high, usually metal, between a fireplace chimney and the upslope of the roof to prevent water and debris from gathering in the cavity.

Cripple A short wall stud to support headers, lintels, window plates, and roof rafters.

Cross-bracing One-by-three pieces of board criss-crossed to support the floor joists. Usually they are placed ten to twelve feet apart.

Curtain wall A partition that does not support an overhead ceiling or roof. Same as nonbearing wall.

d (penny) L. *denarius.* A small coin. The symbol now signifies the length of nails: 8d, 2½ inches long; 16d, 3½ inches; etc. Ask for 8-penny nails.

Damper   A piece of metal in a pipe or flue to control the passage of heat.

Damp-wood termites   Zootermopsis. The largest termite. Lives primarily on dead and decaying wood. Needs much moisture. Fix that leaky shower or toilet.

Darby   A wide board used to smooth concrete.

Decorator's dream   More likely a nightmare. Real estate term.

Deed, or grant deed   A legal document stating ownership of property. The document proves you have title to the property.

Dew point   The temperature at which moisture condenses on a wall or substance. Warm air contains moisture. When it strikes a cold wall the moisture is wrung out; it condenses.

Diagonal bracing   Lumber or steel on a wall at an angle to the vertical side. Not to prevent tipping (that's buttress bracing). See *gusset.*

Dielectric union   Sometimes called insulated union. A nonconducting plumbing fitting used to join pipes made of two different materials to prevent electrolysis.

Differential separation   Won't line up. One side of a crack is at a different level from the other side, or has dropped to a different position.

Doll house   Probably what it says: small, cramped, and overpriced. A real estate term.

Door jamb   See *jamb.*

Down spout   Vertical pipe from gutter. Also called leader pipe. Use them. The more you control water, the better the house.

Drain tile   Pipe used to collect and remove water from earth.

Drip edge   Thin metal edging installed on eaves and rakes to protect the wood from moisture.

Dry rot   Fungus that destroys wood. A misnomer. Should be wood rot.

Dry wall   Interior wall or ceiling covering; usually gypsum board. Has no water in it, unlike plaster.

Dry-wood termites   Kalotermes. Termites that live in wood. Often found in attics.

Duct   Pipe or passageway through which warm air is distributed from the heating plant.

Easement   A right that one may have in someone else's property.

Eave   The portion of a roof that extends beyond the wall.

Efflorescence   Literally means flowering. A white, powdery hydrate that forms on concrete or masonry when moisture is present. The moisture may be behind the wall.

Elbow   An ell. A fitting that makes a turn in a pipe.

Electrolysis   The deterioration of two different metals where they touch, usually found on plumbing pipes.

Electronic filter   Sometimes called electrostatic air cleaners. A super filter that has electrically charged plates. They'll pick up dust and pollen that go through ordinary filters. Good for sufferers of allergies.

Electrostatic air cleaner   See *electronic filter*.

Epoxy   A two-part adhesive used for permanent bonding.

Escrow   Money held by the "holder of the stakes," a third-party company, to pay various people or agencies per instructions.

Fascia   The board covering the end of roof rafters at the eave line.

Fiberglass insulation   Common insulating material that is harmless when installed properly and not disturbed.

Finaled   Permit signed by the governmental inspector, indicating that final inspection has taken place.

Firebox   See *heat exchanger*.

Firebrick   Special brick that can take high temperatures. Used in the firebox area of fireplaces.

Fireclay   A mixture of clay, sand, and cement. Mixed with water, it is used as grout between fireplace bricks in the firebox area.

Fire stop   Solid blocking between wall studs halfway up a wall. Its purpose is to reduce oxygen in case of fire.

Flashing   Tar paper or metal used for waterproofing where walls and roof meet, or around windows, chimneys, vents, and valleys.

Floor furnace   Gravity heating system without the ducts.

Flue   A pipe or chamber to carry gases; a chimney. You'll get sick if you have a faulty one.

Footing   The bottom portion of a foundation. The footing is usually wider than the foundation for better weight distribution.

Forced-air furnace   A furnace that forces heat through ducts by a fan and motor.

Foreclosure   Legal proceeding in which a loan company takes back the house when payments have not been met.

Formaldehyde   A colorless, odorless gas that can cause skin rashes, breathing problems, watery eyes, and burning in the eyes, nose, and throat. Emitted by some construction materials. See *UFFI*.

Foundation   Whatever supports the house that is in contact with earth. Concrete is best. If concrete, the foundation includes the footing.

Full disclosure   Any fault known by seller must be revealed. Agents must inform buyer if he or she knows of such faults.

Fungicide   A poison used to kill or retard growth of fungus. It's poisonous to other things too, so be careful.

Fungus   A mold that destroys wood. It has to have moisture to grow, so beware.

Furnace duct wrap   Insulation for heating ducts and pipes. It may contain asbestos.

Furring   Strips of lumber used as a base to bring a wall out to a desired position. If a wall is uneven, or a pipe projects too far, you "fur out" to get beyond the highest portion, then add the finishing material.

Fuse box   See *service panel.*

Gable   The portion of a roof that goes from the eave line to the ridge or top in an unbroken plane. It has to go back down again to make a true gable. That makes the roof double-sloped.

Girder   Beam. Usually wood, to support loads without close vertical posts. Generally beneath floors.

Glue lam   Laminated wooden beam made up of several pieces of wood glued together.

Grade   Earth level. In termite parlance, earth and grade are the same thing.

Gravity furnace   Heat rises through ducts without a fan. No motor, no filter. Good system.

Ground-fault circuit interrupter (GFCI)   A safety device that monitors the difference between current flowing through the hot and neutral wire. If there is an imbalance of current greater than five milliamps, the current will be cut off instantly. The GFCI measures for electric current leakage.

Grounding   House wiring connected to a buried metal pipe or a copper coated rod embedded in the ground to protect the house and occupants from shocks, electrical fires, and damage to electrical appliances.

Grout   The visible mortar between joints of tile or bricks. It is often colored to blend or contrast with tile.

Gusset   Literally, armpit. In building, it's a triangular plywood brace secured at post and beam joints to prevent side movement.

Gutter   A metal, wood, or plastic trough along the eaves that catches and carries off rainwater, preventing drainage problems.

Gypsum board   Dry wall. Four foot wide panel made of a noncombustible gypsum core encased in paper products.

Hairline crack Minor crack, caused from shrinking or slight house movement.

Header Lumber spanning door or window opening. Same as lintel. Also refers to bricks turned on their ends to form the header course (every five to six courses) in a brick wall.

Hearth The portion of a fireplace on which the fire is built. It often extends into the room, level with the base of the firebox.

Heat exchanger The metal surrounding the burners in a furnace. Sometimes called a firebox.

Hip In building it is a type of roof that has four surfaces; the ends are triangles, the other two sides slope up to the gable, making truncated triangles.

Homestead A home or property protected by law against certain debts. The old meaning of "homestead" is not used much any more. Check into homesteading your house.

Horsefeathers Long, thin strips of wood, wedge-shaped, to lay along the ends of a shingle or shake roof to smooth it out before applying asphalt shingles.

Hot conductor Service-panel wire wrapped in colored insulation. Each one should be individually attached to a fuse or circuit breaker. See *neutral conductor*.

Hydronic furnace Forced—hot water heating.

Individual grounding An electrical outlet that has a third wire, which connects to a ground device.

Insulated union See *dielectric union*.

Insulated windows Two or more panes of glass with a dead-air space between them.

Insulation Everybody knows what insulation is. See *R-value*.

Interceptor drain A ditch cut into a hillside on an angle to collect water and direct it away from your house.

Interior zoning The work, privacy, and shared activity areas of a house.

Intertherm A perimeter-type heater with a sealed-in liquid that heats grills and convects heat. Also called liquid electric.

Jack rafters Short rafters that extend from wall plates to hip or valley rafters.

Jack studs Short studs beneath window plates.

Jamb The wood framing on either side of a door.

Joist Lumber laid on edge to support floor or ceiling.

Knob-and-tube wiring Type of electrical wiring found in older houses. Individually insulated strands of wires threaded through porcelain tubes.

Leach field Part of a domestic sewage system that distributes partially treated waste water over a large area of ground, where bacteria in the soil complete the purification process. See *septic tank.*

Lead A metallic element used especially in pipes, cable sheaths, batteries, solder, and some types of paint. Absorbing too much lead, especially in infants and young children, can cause brain damage. Use of lead in homes is now strictly regulated.

Leader pipe Vertical pipe leading from gutters. Also called downspout.

Lintel Heavy piece of metal that supports the bricks over the fireplace opening. Also see *header.*

Lien A claim on the property of another as security against the payment of a debt.

Liquid electric See *Intertherm.*

Mantel A shelf above the fireplace on which to set clocks or various dust collectors. Used seasonally to display Christmas cards.

Mastic Glue or paste. Used for cementing tile, linoleum, wood, and wood products.

Mineral deposits Impurities in water and rust from steel pipes that form on interior of water pipes. This can be hastened by electrolysis. Use insulated unions.

Molding Finish wood in various shapes used for decorative purposes and to hide mistakes. "Cover it up with molding."

Mortgage A written instrument showing that certain property has been used as security for loan of money. They're okay when you need them but make the happiest fire when returned.

Mud Concrete mortar. Base for installing ceramic tile in showers.

Mullion The vertical divider between window or door glass.

Muntin The strip separating panes of glass.

Neutral conductor Service-panel wire wrapped in white insulation. Should be attached to one metal block. See *hot conductor.*

Nonbearing wall See *curtain wall.*

Nonmetallic sheathed cable Very popular and widely used. Lightweight, easy to install plastic covered conductors.

Nosing Metal strip around the edge of the roof.

Nosing tile Curved tile at the edge of a tile wall.

Obligated room   Real estate term. A room that you have to go through to get to another room.

Old-house borers   Wood-destroying insects whose boring larvae make a rasping or ticking sound. Adult eventually leaves behind a ¼-inch oval hole in wood.

Outlet   Convenience outlet, electrical receptacle. Plug a cord in, hope it works.

Oxide inhibitor   Applied to aluminum wiring connections to prevent electrical problems.

Oxygen venting   See *combustion venting*.

Panel ray heater   See *wall heater*.

Parapet   Turned-up edge on a roof.

Peeling paint   Thin film of paint loosening from surface. Usually caused by moisture within the wall.

Penny   See *d (penny)*.

Perimeter foundation   The outside wall of the house; what the house rests on.

Pier   Concrete base to support posts and keep them off the earth.

Pitch   (1) slope. Usually referred to as the incline of a roof. (2) the messy resin from conifers such as fir and pine trees.

Plenum   Literally, full. The large metal box attached to furnace from which heating ducts emerge.

Plumb   Vertical.

Points   In the financial world, 1 to 1½ percent of the amount loaned on the property. Lenders use points for additional funds.

Polyurethane   Plastic insulating board. One of the best.

Powder-post beetles   No friend of antiques. Small beetles that live in wood. They literally turn the wood to powder. Floor joists they love.

P trap   That part of the drain beneath a sink that turns up, then meets another pipe that goes through the wall. The "P" is the lowest portion of pipe. It holds water all the time to prevent sewer gases from entering the house.

Putty   A soft, pliable, and convenient building material.

Rabbet   A groove cut out of the edge or the face of lumber. Usually rectangular.

Radiant heat   The way sunshine heats; it emits heat rays. Heat in a floor or ceiling emits heat to the room. It may be from hot water or electricity.

Radon gas   A natural radioactive gas that seeps into houses from underground uranium deposits. It may contribute to up to 30,000 cancer deaths a year.

Rafters   The sloping timber of a roof to which the roof surface is nailed.

Rails   The top and bottom horizontal wood members in a door. Attached to stiles, which are the vertical members. Also the top and bottom of a stairway, the handrail.

Rake   The edge of a roof opposite the eave. Usually over an end wall.

Receptacle   See *outlet*.

Ridge   The highest point of a gabled or hip roof. Ridge pole is the timber on which the rafters rest on a gabled roof.

Rise   The height of a step.

Riser   The vertical board at the toe end of each step.

Roll roofing   A less expensive roof covering which comes in rolls. It's secured to the roof with a combination of nails and quick-setting lap cement.

Romex   See *nonmetallic sheathed cable*.

Rust buildup   Particles of rust that form on the inside of steel plumbing pipes. Eventually there is more rust than opening.

Rustic   Usually raw, unpainted exterior. Could be interior. Often referred to as quaint.

R-value   Resistance value. A figure used to signify the insulating value per inch of a product. The higher the R-value, the better the insulation.

Screeds   A guide. Boards placed in position at a level to which concrete is laid. A straight edge reaches from one screed to another and scrapes concrete to level of screeds.

Second mortgage   When a buyer hasn't enough money to pay for a house, either by loan or his or her own cash, a second loan, usually small, is made from some other source. Interest is higher than first mortgage.

Septic tank   Part of a domestic sewage system in which solid wastes are broken down by powerful bacteria, leaving partially treated waste water that flows into a leach field. See *leach field*.

Service panel   Main electric box on house where electric wire from street is connected. Also known as circuit-breaker panel or fuse box.

Shake   A shingle split from a piece of log usually three or four feet long. Used as a roofing material.

Shear strength   The dictionary says tangential movement that prevents movement on a plane, such as a floor. You don't want your floor to move from side to side. Give it shear strength and it won't.

Sheathing   Exterior wall or roof covering. Wall sheathing is often covered by a finish product, like stucco.

Sheetrock   (trademark) Sometimes called dry wall or gypsum board. Two pieces of paper with gypsum between them. Comes in various thicknesses.

Shoe   A quarter-round piece of molding set against the corner where wall meets floor. It goes on top of the finish floor against the baseboard.

Sill   Sill plate. A wood member attached to foundation on which the structure is built.

Sleeper   A wood member sometimes embedded in a concrete slab or laid on the surface, to which the subfloor is attached.

Soffit   The underside of an architectural feature such as a beam, arch, or cornice. The common reference is to the underside of eaves that have been covered with a finishing material.

Sprayed ceiling finish   Spray finish for ceilings that creates a cottage cheese effect. Contains asbestos fibers and was banned in 1977. However, acoustical spray contractors used up their supplies; house ceilings sprayed up to 1982 should be tested.

Square   100 square feet. Roofers use the term most.

Stabilize   To support. To stop or arrest settling or movement.

Stain   A liquid that penetrates wood; usually oil-based.

Stiles   The vertical wood members in a door; attached to the rails.

Straining piece   See *collar beam.*

Stringer   The sides of stairs on which the treads rest.

Strongback   A wood member in an attic area, stretching from one supporting wall to another. Ceiling joists are attached to the strongback to prevent sagging.

Structural fault   A threatening weakness in construction.

Stucco   An exterior wall finish. Composed of cement, sand, lime, and water.

Studs   Vertical members in a wall to which interior and exterior covering are nailed.

Subpanel   Electrical panel installed down line from main service panel to distribute and protect additional circuits.

Subterranean termites   Reticulitermes. Small gray insects, $1/4$ inch long. Live in earth but feed on wood. Do not expose themselves to air. Reach wood by self-made tubes or by earth-to-wood contact.

Summer switch   A switch on a forced-air furnace to operate the fan manually with no heat. A good idea on a hot day.

Sunburned   Roofers' term for shake or wood shingles that have worn thin or completely through.

"Sweetheart" arrangement   A payoff. "As long as you cooperate, I'll give you jobs. But don't forget my percentage."

Tar-and-gravel roof   See *built-up roof.*
Termiticide   An antitermite substance.
Thermocouple   A safety device on most gas- and oil-fired appliances that shuts off the supply of fuel if the pilot light blows out. Commonly found on furnaces and water heaters.
Thermopane   One or more panes of glass with vacuum between. Difficult to replace broken glass; you can't suck that hard. Excellent insulation.
Thermostat   A mechanism to control heat automatically.
Threshold   The bottom of a doorway on which you step or tread to enter or exit.
Title insurance   Insurance on property against claim of ownership by an unknown heir or creditor. A one-time cost. Lasts as long as you own the property.
Toenail   A nail on a slant through one member to another.
Toilet seal   A ring of putty or wax between the toilet and the floor. Don't try to get along without it.
Tread   Stair step.
Trim   Finish material, such as molding. It can cover many sins.

Urea-formaldehyde foam insulation (UFFI)   Insulating material that has been banned in most areas because, though a good insulator, it can give off harmful formaldehyde fumes for years.

Valley   It's the V on roofs where an inside or convex change in roof direction is made. The best valleys have metal in the V.
Vapor barrier   A waterproof covering to prevent moisture penetration. Used on walls and beneath concrete slabs.
V crack   A crack in a foundation that is wider at the top than the bottom and that indicates a serious degree of settling or slippage.
Veneer   Thin pieces of good wood generally used to cover a cheap or poor surface. Brick veneer is genuine, but the bricks are a covering, not bearing.
Vent   A pipe to carry either foul air from an area or fresh air to an area. A furnace vent pipe carries exhaust fumes away.
Volt   Electric power, based on the speed at which electrons travel. 230 volts is more powerful than 115 volts. See *amp* and *watt.*

Wall heater   Space heater, also called panel ray, that works well in added-on rooms.

Watt   The amount of power flowing through a wire. Volts (speed) multiplied by amps equal watts.

Weather-stripping   Material added to door or window frames to prevent passage of air through tiny cracks.

White ants   Common name for termites, though a misnomer.

Wire   See *conductor*.

Wood rot   Same as dry rot, only a more accurate phrase. Deterioration of wood due to growth of fungus.

Wood shingles   Used for roofing. Will last seventeen to twenty-two years in sunny areas, longer where summers are short. Not as thick as shakes.

Zone control heating   Thermostats installed in several sections of a house can keep rooms at different temperatures.

Bibliography

GOVERNMENT PUBLICATIONS, FEDERAL AND STATE, CAN BE OBTAINED FROM THE
U.S. DEPARTMENT OF AGRICULTURE EXTENSION OFFICE IN THE CITY NEAREST
TO YOU.

Basic Housing Inspection. Public Health Service. Publication no. 2123. Superintendent of Documents, U.S. Government Printing Office, Washington, D.C.

Carpentry and Building Construction. U.S. Army TM 5–460. Superintendent of Documents, U.S. Government Printing Office, Washington, D.C.

Coffel, Steve. *But Not a Drop to Drink: The Life-Saving Guide to Good Water*. Rawson, New York.

Condensation Problems in Your House. U.S. Department of Agriculture, Forest Service. Publication no. 373. Superintendent of Documents, Washington, D.C.

Finding and Keeping a Healthy House. U.S. Department of Agriculture, Forest Service. Publication no. 1284 (Termites). Superintendent of Documents, Washington, D.C.

Lafavore, Mike. *Radon: The Quiet Killer*. Rodale, Emmaus, Penn.

Remodelers' Handbook. Craftsman Book Co., 542 Stevens Ave., Solano Beach, Calif. 92075.

Richter, H.P. *Wiring Simplified*. Park Publishing, Box 5527, Lake St. Station, Minneapolis, Minn. 55408.

Roberts, Rex. *Your Engineered House*. J.B. Lippincott Co., Philadelphia.

Wise Home Buying. U.S. Department of Housing and Urban Development. Washington, D.C.

Wood Decay in Houses: How to Prevent and Control it. U.S. Department of Agriculture, Home and Garden Bulletin no. 73. Superintendent of Documents, Washington, D.C.

Yenev, Peter. *Peace of Mind in Earthquake Country*. Chronicle Books, San Francisco, Calif.

Index

About the Authors

The late **George Hoffman** spent thirty years learning, teaching, helping. In 1948 he moved to Sausalito and began to learn about house building by reading, observing, then working with a contractor, and finally by building his own house from the ground up—foundations, construction, plumbing, electricity, roof, and all the myriad extras that crop up as one goes along. The house was built on a small lot 400 yards from an abandoned shipyard. His career as a recycler began with the use of the many materials left in this yard, in the city dump, in old buildings—all the discards of an affluent society. Later he built another house entirely by himself, and then went into remodeling.

When friends asked him to look over houses before they bought, he realized he had a valuable and helpful business before him. This business grew solely by word of mouth. By 1965 he had examined more than 3,500 houses, both for prospective buyers and for owners anxious to keep their property in tip-top shape. He took the buyer or owner with him, diagnosing and explaining the house as he inspected. George Hoffman also taught home inspection in an adult education course at the College of Marin. He was a frequent guest on radio shows, answering questions about houses, and often gave talks on home inspection and maintenance.

Mark C. Friedman is a building inspector in Petaluma, California. While growing up in Sausalito, he grew to know George Hoffman well, and took on the task of updating this book with great respect. He teaches courses in construction at Santa Rosa Junior College.